SUSTAINABILITY METRICS AND MANAGEMENT

SUSTAINABILITY METRICS AND MANAGEMENT

THE PATH FROM INNOVATION TO ROUTINE

STEVEN COHEN,
WILLIAM EIMICKE,
AND GUO DONG

COLUMBIA UNIVERSITY PRESS
NEW YORK

Columbia University Press
Publishers Since 1893
New York Chichester, West Sussex
cup.columbia.edu

Copyright © 2026 Columbia University Press
All rights reserved

Cataloging-in-Publication data is available from the Library of Congress.

ISBN 9780231220668 (hardback)
ISBN 9780231220675 (paper)
ISBN 9780231563352 (epub)
ISBN 9780231565967 (PDF)

Cover design: Noah Arlow
Cover image: Shutterstock

GPSR Authorized Representative: Easy Access System Europe,
Mustamäe tee 50, 10621 Tallinn, Estonia, gpsr.requests@easproject.com

FROM STEVEN COHEN:

TO MY DREAM OF A SUSTAINABLE FUTURE FOR MY GRANDDAUGHTERS LILY, NOA, ADI, AND YAEL . . .

FROM WILLIAM EIMICKE:

TO KAREN, ANNEMARIE, NUGGET, AND ARROW

FROM GUO DONG:

TO QIN HONG AND GUO YINGGUANG

CONTENTS

PREFACE

Every student of management knows that performance measurement is an essential element of effective management. To paraphrase the great management scholar Peter Drucker, you can't manage something if you can't measure it.[1] Without measures, you can't tell if management's actions are making things better or worse. Some managers don't believe this. They believe their decisions should be guided by experience, judgment, and gut instinct. Our view is that guessing is not a good substitute for data. Experience and judgment are required to interpret data, but without performance data, they cannot be applied to the reality an organization confronts.

This brings us to sustainability metrics: a new and evolving field of study still being solidified. Despite their sheer number, we are still in the early days of developing and standardizing these measures. Originally, we emphasized environmental sustainability and those metrics that focused on the physical inputs to an organization, such as energy and water, and the pollution created by the organization's work processes, supply chains, and outputs. These elements lend themselves to hard measures such as:

- The source, amount, and efficiency of energy, material, and water use;
- The organization's impact on biodiversity and air quality and its effluent discharges, including greenhouse gas emissions; and
- Other measures of the physical dimensions of environmental sustainability.

Over the past decade, we have developed increasingly sophisticated measures and methods of estimating greenhouse gases. In Columbia's Master of Science in Sustainability Management program, where two of us teach, we even offer a course in greenhouse gas measurement, along with another analytic course in life cycle assessment. These courses focus on the measurement of the physical dimensions of sustainability.

But the definition of sustainability management has expanded over the past decade or so and has come to include nonenvironmental factors. We have added social impacts and organizational governance to the definition of sustainability. This is sometimes called environmental, social, and governance (ESG) management. In addition to environmental impacts, sustainability management now includes diversity, equity, and inclusion, or what we term fair and inclusive hiring and governance, and the relationship of the organization to the communities it operates in. Organizational governance focuses on the diversity of life experiences and viewpoints present in corporate boardrooms and management. This is often translated into measures of race, gender, and ethnicity, although we believe these demographic measures are inadequate. Diversity should not be seen as the personal characteristics you are born with but as the diverse life experiences of individual managers, staff, and board members.

Community impact can be operationally defined as the relationship and trust the organization has with its host communities. These nonphysical factors are more complex to measure and manage than environmental sustainability. Nevertheless, an organization's ability to compete in a global, brain-based economy depends on its ability to attract the best and brightest people to the organization. Any biases based on race, gender, sexual orientation, religion, or nation of origin limit the pool of talent the organization can attract and can impair its competitiveness. The opposite of diversity, equity, and inclusion is homogeneity, inequity, and exclusion. Similarly, organizations that do not cultivate their host community can find themselves engaged in political battles that impede operations.

These broader concepts of organizational sustainability must be measured and then integrated alongside measures of environmental sustainability in an effort to manage organizations strategically while ensuring operations do as little damage to the planet as possible. The first step in accomplishing this is to integrate these sustainability measures into an organization's key performance indicators and performance measurement system. Sustainability measures must be included with the other nonfinancial indicators of performance and then analyzed to determine their contribution to financial indicators of success. All sustainability measures are not created equal. Some will be more important to individual organizational success than others, so they must be assessed to determine which will become key performance indicators and integrated into the organization's overall performance measurement and management system. These key indicators will vary by organization.

Once sustainability indicators are understood and utilized, it becomes possible to integrate sustainability management into routine organizational management. All organizations have distinct financial units to provide data on financial trends and performance to senior management. They collect financial data from operating units, analyze those data, and help senior management understand the operational factors contributing to financial success or failure. The units responsible for an organization's sustainability performance will collect data from operating units to measure sustainability performance, assess the causes of organizational sustainability success and failure, and then work with the organization's financial unit to determine how these sustainability indicators contribute to financial success and failure.

The ideological and nonmanagerial elements of sustainability management can create difficulties for sustainability management. They have created an impression in conservative political circles that sustainability management is some kind of "woke" form of management that requires politically correct behavior and language that is unrelated to organizational performance.[2] This ideological strain of sustainability is not a right-wing fantasy—it exists—but in this book, we put forward a managerial definition because we believe these factors are increasingly important to managers in the twenty-first century. Organizations operate in an increasingly complex physical, demographic, political, social, cultural, technological, and economic environment. Many of the variables influencing an organization's success or failure are outside of its control, but where these factors can be understood and accommodated or influenced, they should be. We have seen many organizations operate under the mistaken belief that they can muscle their way through a community's opposition only to find after a lot of time and effort that they've come up empty. Local politics prevents them from operating as they hoped.[3] As for environmental sustainability, the field of industrial ecology has already demonstrated that even service organizations can reduce costs by paying attention to their use of energy and water and by modernizing their methods of waste disposal.[4]

The final area where sustainability metrics are becoming more important is in the reporting and management of environmental risk. We are starting to see mandatory reporting requirements for carbon disclosure. The state of California, the European Union, and the US Securities and Exchange Commission (SEC) are in the process of mandating clearly defined corporate carbon disclosures. In the case of the SEC, at some point in the future, these will sit alongside financial disclosures and influence access to and success in public capital markets.[5] Although the SEC rule has been stalled during the second Trump administration, our view is that this type of reporting will eventually be required by the US national government, even if it is first required by some American states and foreign governments. The first generally accepted sustainability metrics will be the greenhouse gases modeled as part of these mandated corporate carbon disclosures. Investors will be able to compare corporate carbon footprints. It is unlikely that they will be satisfied with these indicators alone but will also ask for indicators of exposure to climate impacts and other environmental risks. Corporate exposure to environmental liability will also eventually be measured, and when all these risk factors are added to carbon disclosure, investors and public policymakers will be able to measure an organization's environmental sustainability performance alongside its financial performance.

Understanding environmental risk is necessary to understand financial risk. In a complex, rapidly changing technological environment, it is dangerous for managers or investors to be ignorant of these elements impacting organizational performance. Sophisticated management must be capable of understanding and navigating this complexity. This requires the development of sustainability metrics along with modes of analysis that can relate variation in these metrics to organizational financial success.

The transition to an environmentally sustainable economy will come as we learn how to develop wealth while carefully stewarding our planet's fragile and sometimes scarce resources. Renewable resources like solar power and everything that grows due to photosynthesis, in contrast to finite resources, will enable growth, along with a circular economy that reuses resources rather than burning them or dumping them in a hole in the ground.[6] A key step in developing the management capacity to build this new economy is to create meaningful, actionable sustainability metrics. That process is well underway.

The importance of sustainability management requires the development of generally accepted sustainability metrics. Just as financial accounting requires agreement on terms and reporting requirements to facilitate independent auditing, sustainability requires the same level of precision. Publicly traded and owned corporations are under pressure from investors to report environmental risks, and an increasing number of companies are disclosing ESG measures. Despite the need for reporting, many companies are having difficulty managing this new function. Moreover, some of the early efforts to measure ESG focus on symbolism, statements, and reports on processes rather than organizational outputs and outcomes.

The challenges in reporting are due to imprecise measures and a lack of experience collecting and reporting these data. Those challenges will be met by sustainability professionals trained in measuring greenhouse gases and conducting life cycle analyses. Assuming the SEC rules eventually survive the ideological onslaught now underway, it is likely, just as with financial accounting, that an American rule would be highly influential and, over time, would become a global standard. Although America's right wing has come to dominate the debate over disclosure and the Trump administration has withdrawn the SEC proposal entirely, US corporations operating globally will still be subject to foreign or global reporting requirements that they have little hope of influencing.[7] The realpolitik of sustainability reporting requirements may eventually convince American corporations to focus their attention on influencing rather than overturning reporting requirements. The investor demand for uniform reporting and metrics will remain, and the power vacuum will be filled one way or another.

The initial SEC rule was more limited than many of the other frameworks under development and focused narrowly on carbon disclosure. Our view is that even this now discarded initial rule should be seen as a foot in the door and, like financial accounting, will evolve over time. A growing number of publicly traded companies and even many privately owned companies are disclosing sustainability metrics. The ideologues labeling this as "woke" management fail to understand the degree to which these measures are indicators of effective and sophisticated management. ESG measures do not drive out financial indicators; in fact, they are at times correlated with financial success. The principal concerns of a private firm do not change under sustainability management. They remain profit, market share, and return on equity. But modern organizations recognize that they are operating on a more crowded, interconnected, and warming planet. These facts of organizational environments require that they manage their environmental, social, and community impacts as a part of routine organizational life.

In addition, modern organizations compete for talent, and that means that workers have influence over management behavior. Employees, particularly younger ones, care about a company's ESG performance. The postpandemic push for hybrid work arrangements is ample evidence that top-down management is no longer possible and organizations must respond to employee preferences.

Corporations operate in a regulated environment. That is why they have in-house counsel and engage outside law firms on a regular basis. When white collar employees are fired or laid off, it is not unusual for them to sue their ex-employer. An American corporation operating nationally must understand state law and even local ordinances to successfully function. Companies operating globally must understand the rules of other nations. Over 10,000 non-European companies are subject to the European Union's new ESG reporting requirements.[8] About a third—or over three thousand—are US corporations.[9] This regulatory environment is normal, expected, and fully integrated into decision-making in modern corporations. The free market is a relative and not absolute concept. There has never been and will never be a totally free market because that is akin to anarchy. An indicator of a successful company is its ability to navigate its regulatory environment while achieving its financial goals. The widespread and growing voluntary disclosure of sustainability metrics is happening in anticipation of government regulation but also in response to investor, customer, and employee demands.

However, the problem with voluntary disclosure is that the measures they use do not enable investors to compare one company's environmental risk to another, and the disclosures are not audited. Even worse, some of the nongovernmental organizations (NGOs) that help companies measure and report sustainability are paid by the companies they report on, so these ESG reports might be fiction and we'd never know. Uniform disclosure metrics are urgently needed. In the United States, only the SEC, with its gatekeeper function to the public capital marketplace, has the power to develop and impose standard reporting and audit requirements. Our view is that, eventually, these reporting requirements will reemerge in the US SEC.

Sustainability metrics and, indeed, sustainability management have finally arrived. For those of us who have been working for well over a decade to develop these practices and this profession, this is welcome but not a surprise. The climate crisis modeled and predicted in the final decade of the twentieth century is now with us.[10] The biodiversity loss feared has also arrived.[11] We believe that we can develop a productive and growing economy without destroying our home planet. It takes brainpower, ingenuity, and technology but, most of all, our attention and concern. Carbon disclosure is a critical step in carbon management.[12] Standardized sustainability metrics are a crucial step in realizing the vision of sustainability management.

We have always assumed that the assurance of environmental protection, like national security, is a function of government. The goals of private corporations are to generate profit, return on equity, and market share. These are important goals, and encouraging them along with private initiative has helped generate wealth and well-being for billions of people. Corporations are not designed to be instruments of altruism. The government's role is to ensure that private sector goals are achieved legally and without harming employees, the planet, or the public. How, then, do we explain the clear and obvious private sector push for environmental sustainability? The answer is simple. The private sector has at long last figured out that profitability, return on equity, and increasing market share require that corporations pay attention to the risks posed by the natural environment, the impact of their operation on environmental quality, and their parsimonious use of increasingly scarce finite resources. The private sector is not pushing environmental sustainability due to altruism or ideology but because there is money to be made.

Conservative analysts believe that climate disclosure by corporations is some kind of politically correct fever dream. Nonsense. Look at the state of Florida today, and you see the financial impact of climate-accelerated extreme weather.[13] Extreme weather creates incredible destruction and therefore poses a financial risk, but reconstruction also provides economic opportunity. Any investor looking at a company's risk profile would want to know the company's carbon footprint and exposure to the impact of climate change. Investors need carbon disclosure because it is obvious to any sane analyst that decarbonization is the wave of the future. A company that wastes energy or is not analyzing the regulatory environment stimulated by climate change is, by definition, poorly managed. Moreover, renewable energy is already less expensive than fossil fuels, and soon, it will be more reliable and convenient as well. A company that is not working to reduce its use of fossil fuels is not serious about cost containment or efficiency. Some of the pressure for climate disclosure is coming from the same people who want transparent and audited financial disclosure: careful investors.

Well-managed, forward-looking companies and communities don't need government rules and incentives to convince them to work for environmental sustainability, but not all companies are well-managed or forward-looking. Neither are states and communities. That is why we need rules, regulations, and public policy—to push along those who need pushing and punish those who violate the law. But still, it is remarkable how many companies are reading the handwriting on the wall and know that we are heading to a fossil fuel–free future. The best example of this is in the motor vehicle industry. In the summer of 2023, California announced it would ban the sale of the internal combustion engine in 2035.[14] General Motors also announced it would only sell electric vehicles starting in 2035.[15] It's surprising but not a coincidence. Despite slowdowns in the speed of transition to electric vehicles, they remain the technology of the future. Of course, the action of California's state government banning the sale of internal combustion engines wholly depends on the market and technology of 2035. If people still want to buy internal combustion engines in 2035, either California will need to change its rule or it risks seeing auto sales migrate out of state.

Competent corporate management requires effective environmental sustainability management. Pollution is waste, and waste costs money. Moreover, in an increasingly crowded planet, waste disposal has become expensive, and disposing of your waste in a way that harms your neighbor could end up costing a polluting company billions of dollars. There are scores of examples of companies that have learned the hard way: from the billion dollars that General Electric paid to clean up PCBs in the Hudson River[16] to the many billions BP paid after their disastrous spill in the Gulf of Mexico[17] to Volkswagen's painful lesson when they lied about emissions from their vehicles, losing billions in penalties, lower sales, and lost equity.[18]

It's true that companies hoping to attract brainpower need to be able to defend their impact on the planet when recruiting talent. Many people working in private corporations like to breathe healthy air and hope their children will inherit a planet that is habitable. They are attracted to well-managed, environmentally conscious companies. Similarly, companies that are hospitable to a diverse workforce will have a larger and, therefore, more talented labor pool to draw on, and companies that have good relations with their neighbors will have a greater probability of generating community support should they wish to expand.

But one could argue that these longer-term considerations sometimes take a back seat to the immediate need for profit, return on equity, and market share. That is unquestionably true, and that is why the government must create a regulatory floor below which corporations cannot sink. We would never argue against maintaining and enforcing environmental standards, but we are impressed these days by the number of private, nonprofit, and governmental organizations promoting environmental sustainability.

Over 90 percent of Standard and Poor's top 500 companies now produce annual sustainability reports. According to the Governance and Accountability Institute (G&A), an ESG consulting firm: "G&A's annual research series began nine years ago with the analysis of sustainability reporting activities for publication year 2011, when we found just about 20 percent of the S&P 500 companies were publishing a sustainability report. G&A has found the volume of reporting has steadily increased each year since 2011 and the contents of the reports dramatically expanded over time. By 2012, more than half (53 percent) of the companies were publishing reports. That percentage grew to 75 percent by 2014 and to 86 percent by 2018."[19]

Some of this reporting is clearly greenwashing, but it is an indication of a growing trend in private-sector management. With the European and California carbon disclosure rules now in place, many corporations will eventually be reporting their climate risk and carbon footprint, and these disclosures will help steer capital toward more environmentally sound companies.

Building the organizational capacity to measure, analyze, and report a company's environmental impact is a necessary but not sufficient condition to reduce that impact. The next step is to build the capacity to reduce impact through changes in work processes and/or technologies. General Motors, along with many other manufacturers and service organizations, is building these capacities.[20] These operational changes will make it possible for us to grow our economy while reducing our impact on the planet that sustains us. This is how environmental sustainability will move from talk to operational reality: from words to deeds.

The question of who a good manager is or what is at the core of good management has been asked repeatedly by organizations, individuals, and academics. Although the answer to this question is highly subjective, some things are clear. In order to be able to manage well, one needs data and the ability to assess it. Organizations operate in a complex physical, demographic, political, social, cultural, technological, and economic environment. Many of the variables influencing an organization's success or failure are outside of its ability to control or influence, but where these factors can be understood and accommodated or influenced, they should be. This brings to light the importance of performance measurement and, more crucially, its flexibility.

A concept that has been integrated into performance measurement in the past few decades is environmental metrics—the physical impacts of an organization's operations. However, as noted earlier, over the past decade, a new area of study has materialized: sustainability metrics. These metrics include environmental metrics but also nonenvironmental measures of organizational sustainability. They are often referred to as ESG metrics and DEI (diversity, equity, and inclusion) metrics. These sustainability metrics should be tailored to the organization's needs and objectives and integrated as key performance indicators, with the goal of facilitating a competitive business environment that will attract the right employees, clients, and partners.

To promote a more sustainability-centered managerial approach, it's imperative to fully comprehend how to quantify and analyze the potential of sustainability issues on business performance. To do so, this book will introduce a number of concepts:

1. Sustainability metrics and their influence on performance metrics and financial management
2. Sustainability, DEI, and community impact in management (because of the ideological baggage attached to the term DEI, we will at times term this fairness and inclusiveness)
3. Measuring and assessing sustainability risk

This book is aimed at providing the reader with a detailed definition of sustainability metrics and how they influence sustainability management in a world characterized by constantly changing technologies, economies, political regimes, and cultural phenomena. It explains in detail various facets of the measurement process required to produce reliable and verifiable sustainability metrics and discusses its immediate and direct impact on financial performance. Most importantly, this book gives readers the tools and understanding needed to push their organizations forward in a sustainable and community-conscious manner. The book is divided into seven chapters, summarized below.

Chapter 1: Performance Measurement and Performance Management

The first chapter defines performance measurement and performance management and expands on their centrality in various levels of management. It goes on to explain the reasoning behind the importance of measurement to management and provides alternatives to it. Performance management aims to effectively implement strategies and achieve objectives, whereas performance measurement aims to track the progress of implemented strategies. Measurement and management follow each other in an interactive process.

Chapter 2: Sustainability Metrics and the Transition to Sustainability Management

Sustainability management refers to the methods and strategies used by organizations to meet their sustainability goals, whereas sustainability metrics involve tracking progress toward sustainability using different methods and frameworks. Sustainability management goals comprise the integration of environmental, social, and economic aspects of a company. The sustainability task of an organization involves reducing the negative impacts generated by that organization and possibly generating positive external impacts as well. The environmental goal is to reduce organizational waste and environmental impacts and increase utilization of renewable resources, thereby generating greater efficiency and more revenue per unit of expenditure.

Sustainability metrics aim to measure the state of performance through the measure of environmental impact, organizational diversity of perspectives, and community impact. Different metrics are relevant for different organizations according to their respective impact on society and the environment. Assessment of climate risk is an emerging environmental metric due to investors' concerns about the effects of climate change on revenue generation and expenses in response to damage due to climate change. Other sustainability metrics include water usage, energy consumption, carbon emissions, waste diversion, and so on.

Chapter 3: Integrating Sustainability Metrics Into Performance Management and Financial Performance

Chapter 3 addresses methods of integrating sustainability metrics into an organization's performance management system and connecting these measures to the organization's financial performance. Whereas traditional metrics focus on immediate financial and operational results, sustainability metrics measure factors that enhance longer-term or indirect results. Sustainability metrics address the environmental, social, and governance aspects of business that are crucial for quality assurance, risk management, and operational security. This integration process involves considering factors like stakeholder expectations, legal requirements, industry norms, and how well these sustainability goals align with the organization's strategic objectives. The chapter also addresses the difference between short-term and long-term as well as direct and indirect measures in defining success. Real-life examples are provided to show how organizations have integrated sustainability into their performance evaluations, highlighting the benefits and costs of such practices. We demonstrate how sustainability factors have been added to performance measures and annual performance reports.

Chapter 4: Integrating Sustainability Management Into Organizational Management

Chapter 4 explores the process of integrating sustainability management into the core of organizational management, which is expected to drive a transformative approach to organizational operations. We detail the benefits of more mindful community engagements, more transparent organizational governance, and more thoughtful production processes designed to reduce negative environmental impacts. We discuss how this integration offers organizational benefits by contributing to long-term positive societal trends and meeting the growing expectations of stakeholders for responsible environmental and community stewardship. Sustainability practices change across organizational practices and departments, so it is important to understand how the application of sustainability performance varies according to organizational goals. The chapter offers an evaluation of common challenges faced by organizations when integrating sustainability into routine organizational management, how to overcome them, and how to leverage sustainability as a competitive advantage. It provides an overview of three case studies on organizations that have succeeded in integrating and "normalizing" sustainability management.

Chapter 5: Environment, DEI, Transparent Organizational Governance, and Community Impact: Ideology and Management Competence

Chapter 5 addresses the broadened conceptualization of sustainability, going beyond the conventional environmental focus to incorporate aspects of diversity, equity, transparent governance, and community impact or fairness and inclusiveness. Although many critics of sustainability consider it to be ideological and not related to organizational management, this chapter builds the management case for this broader definition of sustainability and considers its inclusion central to the definition of competent and effective management. Environmental sustainability remains a critical element of sustainability management, but there is a management case for these nonphysical dimensions of sustainability as well.

In a global, brain-based economy, an organization that reflects non-talent-related biases when hiring and promoting staff reduces its talent pool. Sexism, homophobia, xenophobia, and racism eliminate talent and reduce the organization's ability to compete. Senior management and organizational governance that are homogenous eliminate multiple perspectives and life experiences from the management process. This increases the probability of flawed strategy and decision-making.

Finally, an organization that ignores its impact on its host community runs the risk of generating political opposition to expansion plans and difficulty in recruiting key staff. This chapter makes the case that more mindful and careful management tends to be more effective and competent management. An organization that abuses its host community will typically generate unpredictable and negative responses. A well-managed organization will work to avoid negative environmental and community impacts.

Chapter 6: Measurement and Disclosure of Carbon and Climate Risks

Chapter 6 addresses the growing demand by stakeholders for climate and environmental risk disclosure. It discusses the now-deferred rulemaking of the US SEC and other global trends in regulations, such as the advancements established by the European Union Corporate Sustainability Due Diligence Directive (CSDDD). It includes a description of available approaches to directly and indirectly measure greenhouse gas emissions, including Scopes 1, 2, and 3, and how to report greenhouse gas measures.

Chapter 6 also addresses measurement frameworks, such as that developed by the Task Force on Climate-Related Financial Disclosures (TCFD), which set standards for companies to report their emissions and climate risks in a consistent and comparable manner across sectors and locations. Companies can also use the methods and guidelines we examine in this chapter to identify and report on climate change–induced opportunities, as well as set internal targets that align with global climate goals and track progress.

Chapter 7: Conclusion: Environmental Risk, Financial Risk, and Effective Management in a Complex, Technological, and Global Economy

This concluding chapter examines the relationship between environmental risk, financial risk, and management effectiveness in today's complex, technology-driven global economy. It highlights the challenges faced by modern organizations, including the effects of globalization, rapid technological advancements, and changing political landscapes. The chapter emphasizes the growing importance of sustainability metrics and disclosure as key indicators of management performance. It presents a compelling case for the integration of environmental and financial risk management as a cornerstone of successful organizational strategy and management.

SUSTAINABILITY METRICS AND MANAGEMENT

1

PERFORMANCE MEASUREMENT AND PERFORMANCE MANAGEMENT

Sustainability metrics and sustainability management developed from a long history of performance measurement and performance management in business, government, and the social sector in the United States and around the world. Those familiar with the subject immediately think of the Einstein of management science, the late Peter Drucker, as well as the private sector's profit-motivated drive to constantly produce goods and services better, faster, and cheaper. For managers in the public sector, a common association with performance management is elected officials urging public servants to do more with less. The social sector's commitment to keep overhead expenses below 10 percent is a widely recognized expression of a commitment to an ever-higher level of performance. Our view is that performance management aims to effectively implement strategies and achieve objectives, whereas performance measurement aims to track the progress of implemented strategies. Measurement and management are connected to each other in an endless interactive process. This chapter introduces the management concepts and practice of performance measurement and management, which is the area of management the rest of the book explores as the subfields of sustainability metrics and sustainability management are addressed.

Although Peter Drucker deserves much of the credit for spreading the gospel of performance management as a business strategy, performance measurement emerged as a tool to assess government effectiveness. In the 1930s, Nobel Laureate Herbert Simon and his mentor Clarence Ridley developed a system to evaluate the effectiveness of municipal government and report their findings to the public, most notably in New York City. Simon and Ridley focused on local government outcomes and the efficiency of achieving those outcomes so that citizens could better decide whether they were getting sufficient value for the taxes they paid. They emphasized that the public should be informed on a regular basis using easy-to-understand language so that some level of accountability could be achieved.

Several decades later, Drucker would put performance and accountability at the center of management's responsibility. Drucker argued management's key function is to make work more productive by enabling workers to do more and holding them accountable for doing so. He also believed that Total Quality Management (TQM) provided a process through which workers and management could collaborate to achieve better outcomes in less time and at a lower cost per unit.

In the twenty-first century, the digitization of data, voice, and visual information combined with artificial intelligence (AI)-assisted computer capacity to access, analyze, and draw actionable conclusions have created the potential for dramatic improvements in organization management and thereby improve its outcomes and impacts. Today, there is a wealth of information on virtually every aspect of organizational operations. Leaders and managers must determine which data is directly connected to improved performance and what tools they can most effectively deploy to hold their members accountable for achieving a higher level of impact.

Globalization of the economy through major advances in communication, transportation, and automation has made it possible for businesses to locate almost anywhere and sell to almost anyone. Countries must compete for private-sector jobs, and therefore, the quality of governance, public infrastructure, and rule of law are key elements in the decision on where to locate a business. The internet and smartphones help put social sector organizations in a global competition for donors. Access to information about world events drives donors and social organizations to help not only locally but also globally. Organizations, no matter the sector, must perform at a world-class level if they expect to survive and prosper. And, as Drucker so often said, the most important measure of good management is performance.

BUILDING A COMPREHENSIVE PERFORMANCE MANAGEMENT SYSTEM

How does senior management go about reaching a world-class level of performance? Many ingredients go into organizational success—great people, goods and services that customers value, sound finances, a clear mission, and a multiyear strategic plan. To ensure that the organization is on the right path and stays on it while moving at a brisk pace, a robust information and performance management system is essential. Building an effective performance management system begins with three foundational steps: benchmarking, defining success and developing measurable indicators of that success, and building an accountability system to focus the entire organization on its progress in carrying out the organization's mission.[1] That is how we define performance measurement and management.

Benchmarking involves identifying organizations that excel in the aspects of the mission you aim to enhance.[2] In pursuit of achieving an organization's mission and improving customer service, value proposition, efficiency of operations, employee safety, and all the other critical functions, benchmarking seeks to identify organizations regarded as superior in those activities. Best practices may be found in competitors but might also come from organizations in another field or sector (e.g., government, for-profit, or social sector organizations). Many organizations use benchmarking to learn and improve their efficiency and results.[3]

One of the most successful examples of benchmarking is the McDonald's Corporation's application of the basic principles of Ford

Motor Company's assembly line system for automobile production to the food service industry. The McDonald's "speedy system" created an environment where food could be quickly served to customers when speed was a major issue in the food industry. McDonald's created its own machinated kitchen production line with a specialized crew focusing on one specific task and many initial parts of the menu items coming preassembled, allowing for streamlined food preparation while new orders come in. This process is very similar to the historic Ford manufacturing system, which allowed the mass production of vehicles, cutting down unit price and increasing per-capita efficiency while significantly increasing output. For McDonald's, the product itself, in this case mainly the burger, is standardized with a simple recipe and predetermined quantity of each part, making quality consistent, cutting down unnecessary labor, and increasing output while reducing service speed.

Similarly, government agencies involved in customer-facing work such as issuing and renewing driving licenses and car registrations, receiving fines, and issuing passports and visas have copied private business models of online processing. What used to take up to an entire day of waiting in a government office can now be completed online in minutes at home or even on a mobile phone. Benchmarking enables organizations to discover new operating processes to accomplish their mission in a measurably more effective way.

Defining success is crucial to an organization's survival. The organization's strategic plan must define success and present a series of projects or tasks designed to achieve success now and at least several years into the future. The performance management system must identify the activities that lead to success and measure progress over time. In practice, creating the optimal mix of measurable indicators may vary widely by sector, stage of development, and location.

In the private sector, success is often quantified through metrics such as profit, market share, return on capital employed, debt structure, cash flow, cost control, and earnings per share. Social sector organizations typically prioritize the number of people helped, amount of help provided, impact of the assistance, overhead expenses, volunteers recruited, contributions raised, contracts signed, donors acquired and maintained, and even media attention to their work. For government agencies, public safety and security, rule of law, due process, control of corruption, access to healthcare, education, a living wage, school attendance, response times, reduction of inequality, balance of trade, interest rates, employment and unemployment, and the quality of air, water, and social services are just a few of the important components in defining success. Despite these diverse measurement standards, a general framework for evaluating success can be applied using a four-step approach: inputs, work processes, outputs, and outcomes.[4]

Inputs are the resources or supplies allocated to execute a mission, deliver services, or complete a project. These inputs can normally be quantified in terms of time (duration invested in various tasks), financial resources (budgets and expenditures), human capital (skills, expertise, and labor of the personnel involved), information, and assets utilized (both physical resources such as equipment and intangible resources such as technology and intellectual property). In broad terms, input measures quantify how hard the organization is trying to achieve success. Trying hard is not the same as succeeding, but to some extent, the more resources you devote to achieving success, the higher is the probability of success.

Work processes involve the efficiency of the deployment of inputs to the specific activities undertaken to achieve success. Some of the most common work process measures are cost per unit, time to produce each unit of work, error rates, waste, level of quality, variation, and cost savings achieved. Work processes focus on how inputs are systematically transformed into outputs and involve examining the methods and techniques used to achieve these results. They provide insight into operational effectiveness, process optimization, and quality control, ensuring that resources are used effectively and that the intended goals are met with optimal performance and minimal waste. Simply put, work process indicators are designed to measure the management of inputs used in production.

Outputs are the measurable results of the inputs and work process actions. In the private sector, outputs might be quantified by metrics such as units produced, services delivered, capital raised, accounts acquired, or loans made. In the social sector, outputs could include metrics like the number of individuals served, patients treated, meals served, homeless persons sheltered, or food banks supplied. For governments, outputs might be quantified by indicators such as the number of children attending public schools, pieces of mail delivered, people educated, facilities inspected, miles of road paved, potholes filled, tons of garbage collected, criminals arrested, fires fought, ambulance trips, or gallons of water treated and delivered.

Outcomes measure the impact of the outputs. For the private sector, outcome measures may include market share, new customers added, existing customers retained, profits earned, jobs created, taxes paid, or carbon dioxide (CO_2) emissions reduced. In the social sector, outcomes might be assessed in terms of improved quality of life for beneficiaries, reduction in homelessness, fewer hospitalizations, increases in school attendance, declines in obesity, or fewer people in prison. Outcome measures for government organizations might be very similar to those for social sector organizations, including increases in life expectancy, reductions in homelessness, lower crime rates, increases in income, cleaner air and water, increased graduation rates, fewer fires, fewer accidents, increases in population, more tourists, or higher employment and lower unemployment.

In the context of sustainability metrics and sustainability management, long-term success is critically important not only because it benefits the organization but also because it aligns with the United Nations' Sustainable Development Goals and addresses the evolving needs of societal development. Sustainability is conceptualized as the convergence of social, environmental, and economic dimensions—often summarized as people, planet, and profit. This perspective implies that advancing sustainability requires the concerted efforts of organizations across all sectors. Moreover, such endeavors contribute to a more prosperous future, fostering both organizational success and broader societal well-being.

GETTING FROM MEASUREMENT TO MANAGEMENT

Once management has established definitions of success and the metrics for measuring it, they face the critical challenge of ensuring accountability across organizations, contractors, partners, and individuals. This task is inherently complex. If performance targets are set unrealistically high or excessively low, there is a risk that those responsible may either become discouraged or neglect their responsibilities, undermining the effectiveness of the accountability system.[5] To address this, management must ensure that targets are realistic and aligned with actual capabilities and that the performance measurement system accurately reflects desired outcomes. In general, we prefer to measure existing levels of performance and measure improvements in performance rather than set a target. It is essential that all stakeholders are held accountable for their contributions and that mechanisms are in place to monitor progress, address issues, and provide feedback. This approach not only fosters a culture of responsibility but also ensures that all parties are engaged in achieving the organization's goal.

In our experience, it is more productive to hold *teams* accountable for improved performance rather than *individuals*. In addition, to improve current levels of performance throughout the organization, it is beneficial to periodically review the unit that is most successful in improving performance and simultaneously review the least successful unit. The other units and senior management can thereby adopt best practices organization-wide and institute reforms to avoid very low performance levels. The New York City Department of Fire, Disaster, and Emergency Medical Services—FDNY—had great success with this model in the mid-2000s.

As we noted earlier, you cannot effectively manage what you do not measure. Performance measurement is a fundamental requirement of effective management.[6] Measurement is a means to the end or goal of better management. Therefore, we must understand precisely what "performance" means in each specific situation.[7]

A core purpose of management is to provide direction to an organization's human resources. By using performance measurement, managers can assess how effectively employees and teams are performing. Based on the actual outputs and outcomes achieved by employees and teams, managers can reflect on the organization's mission, establish realistic objectives, and allocate resources to achieve the results desired.[8] The utilization of measurement systems serves to diminish the dependence on intuition or guesswork, thus facilitating a more data-driven, fact-based approach to management.[9] By systematically measuring and analyzing performance metrics, managers are equipped with objective insights that enhance management processes, decision-making processes, and strategic planning. This empirical methodology ensures that organizational actions are grounded in concrete evidence rather than subjective assumptions, ultimately leading to improved efficiency and effectiveness in achieving the organization's objectives.

Ideally, an effective performance management system includes a mixture of input, process, output, and outcome measures. Continued success requires ongoing assessments of the resources committed to specific objectives, how efficiently those resources are used, the volume of outputs produced, and the contribution of those outputs to the achievement of the organization's mission. Senior management must consider the importance of the initiative, the context of other important priorities, and the possible negative interactions between the measures chosen. For example, lowering response times for fire trucks and ambulances can lead to an increase in motor vehicle accidents. Reducing variation in products or services could improve quality but also significantly increase per-unit cost.

The metrics chosen, how they are reported, and how they are used to manage the organization are among the most important decisions a leadership team can make. They are the operational definition of success. The metrics chosen convey the organization's priorities. It is also important to consider the number of metrics established. Focusing on too many metrics can dilute the importance of each one and increase the pressure on employees, potentially leading to diminished overall performance. Holding individuals or even divisions accountable for twenty or more "key" indicators may create the impression that each individual metric is not that important, and therefore, the manager may only focus on the ones they themselves deem most relevant or most positive.

Conversely, prioritizing too few metrics may result in employees paying less attention to important aspects of their work. Focusing only on impact measures can lead to the assumption that cost is not a major concern or that efficiency in achieving the desired impact is a secondary concern. Reducing CO_2 emissions is a laudable impact measure, but if it leads to dramatic increases in energy costs and high unemployment, then a more efficient and less costly method of achieving the impact must be considered.

It is essential and not easy to balance the number of metrics to ensure comprehensive performance management without overwhelming employees. Additionally, it is important to be mindful of what is not being measured because this can inadvertently lead to negligence in those areas. Ensuring that employees do not overlook aspects of their work that are not explicitly measured is crucial for maintaining overall effectiveness and achieving organizational goals. For example, the NYC CompStat performance management system is credited with dramatically reducing serious crimes in New York City, but as originally designed, it did not include measures of citizen complaints and evidence of overaggressive policing. Residents welcomed the safer streets but also wanted the police to treat them with respect and minimize conflict as much as possible.

Each performance metric must be closely aligned with the organization's goals and values to avoid misdirecting organizational efforts. Establishing an effective performance measurement system that satisfies the diverse needs and expectations of customers, employees, managers, organizations, and stakeholders is a complex and challenging endeavor. This process requires a strategic approach to ensure that the selected metrics not only reflect the organization's objectives but also promote behaviors and outcomes that are conducive to long-term success.

MODELS OF COMPREHENSIVE PERFORMANCE MANAGEMENT SYSTEMS

Three of the most popular and influential models for performance management systems based on quantitative measures are management by objectives, the balanced scorecard, and key performance indicators. All three continue to influence performance management designers around the globe. Rather than simply choosing one of the three models, it makes more sense to take the parts of each that best fit your organization and your goals.

Management by objectives (*MBO*), introduced by Peter Drucker in 1955, is a management system grounded in the principle of goal congruence to enhance organizational performance. According to Drucker, when all members of an organization direct their efforts toward shared objectives and their contributions are harmonized to create a cohesive and unified effort, it minimizes gaps, reduces friction, and eliminates unnecessary duplication of tasks.[10] At the time of its introduction, this focus on aligning goals was considered one of the most effective strategies for achieving improved profitability and overall organizational success.

Typically, there are six steps in the MBO model[11]: identification of organizational strategy, collaborative goal setting, linking rewards to goals, development of action plans, cumulative periodic review of subordinate results, and review of organizational performance. Step one is identifying your long-term strategic goals, which serve as a benchmark for your employees and the standard by which organizational progress is measured. Next, goals are established through a collaborative process involving leaders, managers, and implementers at all levels and from all divisions of the organization. These goals should be consistent and aligned across all organizational levels to ensure coherence.

According to Drucker, for the MBO framework to be an effective motivational strategy, it is crucial to connect rewards with the goals.[12] Action plans are essential for identifying problem areas, allocating resources effectively, fostering innovation, and empowering employees. It is also helpful to ensure that planning includes both subordinates and their supervisors.

Cumulative periodic reviews of organizational outputs and outcomes keep management up to date on progress toward the designated goals and on unexpected challenges. This enables managers to provide coaching and support when subordinates encounter difficulties. The final step of MBO involves a thorough review of the entire system, which feeds back into the first step. It helps ensure that organizational plans are being executed as intended and that strategic goals remain the central focus, which can help refine and adjust future objectives to maintain alignment with the overall strategy.

The *balanced scorecard* was developed by professors Robert Kaplan and David Norton in 1992. Like MBO, the balanced scorecard links strategic planning to performance management. The methodology organizes performance measures into four categories: financial measures, internal business processes, customer satisfaction, and employee learning and growth. The balanced scorecard measurement system was designed to address what its authors identified as the limitations of traditional performance systems, which often relied predominantly on financial metrics, such as revenues, expenditures, return on investment, profit, and market share.

To counter what the designers believed was an overly narrow and short-term focus, Kaplan and Norton added qualitative measures to the traditional quantitative metrics and sought to include longer-term goals and measures. Evaluating customer satisfaction through surveys, focus groups, and other outreach techniques gathers important information on key external stakeholders. The learning and growth category focuses on an internal stakeholder group—employees. Reminiscent of the total quality management methodology, these measures emphasize empowering workers, investing in their education and professional development, and encouraging their participation in improving work processes. This necessarily involves qualitative, quantitative, short-term, and long-term metrics.

The term *key performance indicators* (*KPIs*) is twenty-first-century shorthand for performance management measures and management, building on the work of Frederick Taylor, Herbert Simon, Clarence Ridley, Peter Drucker, Robert Kaplan, and David Norton. It is not fundamentally different from MBO and the balanced scorecard but rather seeks to be more inclusive and balanced: KPIs include short- and long-term goals; are customer, employee, and management driven; focus more on outcomes than output; and include a healthy dose of total quality management (often called lean management now, even though the terms are essentially synonymous) and a new emphasis on sustainability.

To establish an effective KPI system, a structured approach involving a six-stage process is recommended by proponents. First, secure commitment from the CEO and senior management, which requires their active endorsement and the formulation of a comprehensive KPI development strategy. Second, focus on enhancing internal capabilities to manage the KPI project, necessitating the formation of a proficient KPI project team and the establishment of a proactive culture and process. Third, lead and promote the change by effectively communicating the KPI system to all employees. Fourth, identify the organization's operational critical success factors. Fifth, determine appropriate performance measures, document performance metrics in a database, select relevant team performance measures, and identify organizationally significant KPIs. Finally, leverage these measures to drive performance by developing reporting frameworks at various levels, facilitating the effective use of key KPIs, and continuously refining KPIs to ensure their ongoing relevance.[13] An important purpose of KPIs is to set a limited number of priority or key indicators. Given the proliferation of performance indicators, it is important that management focus on those deemed "key."

The dramatic increase in the digitization of information, including text, voice, and video; the computing capacity to hold all the data; and AI to process and analyze it rapidly is creating new opportunities to predict behavior, anticipate emergencies, and prevent problems before they arise. This enables new KPIs to emerge and ensures that some current indicators will disappear.

The nature of an organization—whether public or private—significantly influences the selection of performance indicators.

Private sector organizations typically adopt a profit-oriented approach when determining KPIs. In contrast, government entities, similar to other public sector organizations, prioritize the effective delivery of goods and services to the public. In addition, KPIs should be chosen to provide a comprehensive summary of the organization's current status and strategic outlook, and there are no absolute constraints on KPI selection other than ensuring their relevance to the specific characteristics of each organization.

Social impact measures are becoming a standard component of some performance management systems. Surveys indicate that younger people rank social value above profit as the primary purpose of business. And many of society's most pressing challenges—climate change, conflict, hunger, education, and affordable healthcare and housing—require contributions from organizations in the private and social sectors, as well as government. Some well-known systems to measure social impact include the disability-adjusted life-year (DALY), the best available charitable option (BACO), the Organization for Economic Cooperation and Development's (OECD) social internal rate of return, the Social Progress Index, the B Impact Assessment, and the most widely known and extensive Global Impact Investing Network (GIIN) developed by the Rockefeller Foundation.[14] For effective sustainability management, we need to develop new technologies and methods to distribute and use water more efficiently, recycle and reuse what is now waste, better regrow and regenerate food, and dramatically expand the production of renewable energy. This will require hiring new employees with special skills, reengineering our material resources use, measuring our organization's environmental impact, and finding ways to reduce our negative impact.

Although all methods aim to improve organizational performance, each employs distinct mechanisms to achieve this end. MBO is more focused on goal setting and reward systems. The balanced scorecard offers a more comprehensive approach by integrating a diverse array of performance metrics that are aligned with strategic objectives, thereby facilitating a balanced view of organizational performance across multiple dimensions. KPIs provide tailored performance metrics that can be customized to fit various organizational contexts, offering flexibility in performance measurement.

Research has shown that well-designed performance management systems can have a beneficial impact on employees, managers, and organizations.[15] Typically, organizations in all sectors do not exist solely for their own sake; their objectives include making specific contributions to individuals, society, and even the future of the world.[16] But improper or overly excessive management may lead to employee resistance and a high labor turnover rate. Management is considered a practice that, while incorporating elements of both science and craft, is fundamentally practical in nature.[17]

A comprehensive portfolio of performance measures should encompass both quantitative and qualitative dimensions. This includes not only objective metrics but also qualitative assessments that capture ethical considerations, emotional well-being, psychological impacts, and the "fit" of organizational culture. Qualitative factors matter because they also strongly relate to the mission and goals of the organization, which can help build a holistic evaluation of performance that goes beyond numerical data.

MEASUREMENT AND MANAGEMENT OF HUMAN RESOURCES

Performance measurement involves the systematic use of quantitative methods and data analysis to assess and describe employees' job performance. It is critical to recognize that "what you measure is what you get."[18] Measure only what you will manage, what is crucial for the job, what is needed for the organization's development, and what will maintain buy-in from stakeholders. Do this while still limiting the number of KPIs.

In human resources, performance measurement has traditionally been a top-down managerial tool. To deal with employee behavior and performance appraisal, both quantitative and qualitative metrics are used with very mixed results. The concept of measurement extends beyond the mere quantification of performance metrics. Measures can be used to influence employee motivation, foster continuous learning, facilitate self-improvement, and provide employees the opportunity to influence their job design.[19] From an employee's perspective, effective measurement serves as a multifaceted tool that contributes to both personal and professional development.

Measurement, when implemented thoughtfully, establishes a baseline for performance comparison over time, thus enabling normal feedback mechanisms. The feedback, when timely and constructive, can significantly boost employees' intrinsic motivation by affirming their competencies and guiding their developmental path.[20] This feedback baseline functions as a reference point against which employees can gauge their progress, providing a clear understanding of their performance relative to organizational standards and peers and information about what they are doing well and what they need to work to improve. This process involves collecting data on various performance metrics, which act as reference points for future evaluations and are crucial for setting personal development goals and fostering motivation, helping to promote a culture of continuous improvement.

Moreover, measurement can be a catalyst for ongoing learning. By identifying performance trends and areas for improvement, employees are encouraged to engage in reflective practices and seek opportunities for skill enhancement.[21] For example, targeted training or development initiatives can be implemented to address specific deficiencies and foster a culture of continuous learning. This continuous feedback loop not only sustains motivation but also facilitates lifelong learning, which is crucial in an ever-evolving work environment. Employees are encouraged to view setbacks as opportunities for growth rather than failures. The goal is to enable staff to perceive measurement as a supportive tool rather than a punitive mechanism.

For management, measurement is a tool for monitoring, controlling, evaluating, and rewarding employees. Additionally, it helps identify employees' training needs, strengths, and weaknesses, ultimately improving organizational effectiveness. Measurement enables managers to set clear, measurable objectives and effectively track progress toward these goals. By establishing specific targets, managers can monitor employee performance and ensure alignment with organizational objectives. This process both facilitates accurate performance evaluations and provides a solid basis for rewarding employees who meet or exceed expectations.[22] In addition, it offers a transparent record of performance that can help managers make informed decisions regarding the continuation or discontinuation of employment, relying on objective performance outcomes rather than subjective evaluations.[23] By recognizing and nurturing talent, organizations can enhance employee satisfaction and retention.

Measurement also helps identify employees' training needs in order to mitigate weaknesses and improve organizational effectiveness. By assessing performance data, managers can pinpoint areas where employees require additional support or development. Measurement can also highlight the strengths of employees, enabling staff and management to leverage these strengths to maximize organizational benefit.[24] For instance, employees who consistently perform well in specific tasks can be assigned to roles or projects that capitalize on their strengths, thereby maximizing their contributions to the organization. By providing a comprehensive understanding of employee performance, managers can make data-driven decisions that enhance overall productivity and efficiency.

Human resources are a vital asset and play a crucial role in the success and mission accomplishment of organizations.[25] The dedication, skills, and commitment of employees and volunteers directly influence the effectiveness of organizations in fulfilling their goals. Performance management and performance measurement are key for ensuring effective human resources management.[26] The aim is to optimize the alignment of human resources to enhance individual performance, ultimately striving to maximize organizational outcomes.[27]

Employees in the nonprofit and governmental sectors often demonstrate a high level of intrinsic motivation and a deep commitment to the mission of their organization.[28] Unlike for-profit sectors where financial gains are typically the primary focus, because of their inherent characteristics, nonprofit and governmental organizations often find it challenging to reward employee performance with financial incentives such as salary raises or bonus payments.[29] Nevertheless, the ability to attract, retain, and develop talented individuals is paramount for all organizations. Therefore, methods of accomplishing these goals without significant individual financial rewards must be developed in the nonprofit and governmental sectors.

Next, we discuss qualitative metrics, which complement these quantitative methods by capturing aspects like employee satisfaction, organizational culture, and customer perceptions. By integrating these qualitative aspects, organizations can access a more holistic view of their performance and enhance their ability to address both tangible and intangible factors that influence overall effectiveness.

QUALITATIVE METRICS

Not every important aspect of an organization's performance can be quantified easily, if at all. Nevertheless, when asked what makes their organization better than their competitors, leaders frequently respond, "It's our people. We have the best employees in the world!" This may not be an outlandish statement, but if the leader is asked to objectively document their claim, it might be difficult, if not impossible, to do so.

There is no question that workers are a key element in organizational performance, and many organizations have rigorous and expensive annual employee performance appraisal systems to assess virtually every one of their members. Generally, these measurement systems are based on an annual set of tasks for the worker established by their supervisor along with some standards by which their performance will be evaluated, often represented by one of five potential scores or grades ranging from poor to outstanding. Typically, both parties sign the assessment plan, and the evaluation includes both written feedback and an in-person meeting.

Unfortunately, there is seldom a connection between this qualitative assessment and performance management. Personnel actions in the public sector are often governed by both civil service laws and rules and union contracts. Therefore, depending on the organizational culture, supervisors grade every employee as great, good, or satisfactory. Unsatisfactory evaluations are often challenged by union representatives and/or trigger a long and paperwork-intensive response process.

In the private sector, evaluations can be taken more seriously, although in larger organizations, the same disconnect between assessment and consequence applies. A notable and well-publicized example of a performance appraisal system with consequences was a core element of Jack Welch's extraordinarily successful term as CEO of General Electric between 1981 and 2001. Known as "Neutron Jack" for what many viewed as his ruthless personnel policies, Welch mandated that managers terminate the bottom 10 percent of their employees every year while rewarding the top 10 percent with significant raises and stock options. Under his leadership, GE's market value grew from $12 billion to $410 billion, and Welch credited much of this growth to his "rank and yank" performance appraisal system. However, over time, as low-performing personnel depart, the bottom 10 percent at some point becomes higher quality and talented staff end up being fired.

Welch also had a PhD in engineering and remained committed to rigorous testing and independent evaluation, even of methods he was sure were effective. Therefore, after about six years of extraordinary success for GE's profits and stock price, he hired an outside firm to evaluate his system, curious to see if the outcomes were as positive as he thought. What they found was that the top 10 percent of performers in the system stayed with the company and prospered. However, the consultant also found that only about a third of the bottom 10 percent should have been terminated.

Moreover, the largest group of employees leaving GE was from the 10 percent of employees just under the top 10 percent of high performers; these employees felt undervalued and found better jobs in other companies. To his credit, Welch modified the system to reward the top 20 percent equally and intervene with the bottom 20 percent to help them improve their performance.

Three other personnel performance appraisal systems have significantly influenced organizations in the public, private, and nonprofit sectors—360-degree feedback, critical incident methodology, and cultural/behavioral assessments. *Three-hundred-sixty-degree feedback systems* are often derived from the work of Mark Edwards, a former US Navy pilot, whose system developed out of the peer review practices in US military organizations.[30] This feedback mechanism is also known as full-circle appraisal, multirater feedback, multisource feedback, upward feedback, group performance review, 360-degree appraisal, 540-degree feedback, all-round feedback, and peer appraisal, all of which convey the same concept.[31] The methods for collecting feedback typically encompass questionnaires (administered in paper-based, online, or digital formats), interviews (conducted via telephone, group settings, or face to face), unstructured interviews, and email communications.

A defining feature of 360-degree feedback is its incorporation of multiple perspectives. This feedback process involves gathering perceptions regarding an individual's behavior and its impact from a diverse range of sources, including supervisors, direct reports, peers, subordinates, project team members, and internal and external customers and suppliers.[32] By integrating these varied viewpoints, 360-degree feedback supports several key areas such as self-development, identification of training needs, teambuilding, performance appraisal, strategic development, and remuneration. Furthermore, it plays a significant role in facilitating cultural change, managing succession planning, optimizing personnel placement, promoting organizational values, and enhancing communication and decision-making processes within the organization.[33]

The implementation of the 360-degree multirater feedback system is expensive and time consuming, particularly for government and social sector organizations.[34] Notably, for many years, Columbia University has incorporated 360-degree feedback analysis into the executive education programs for the next generation of leaders of New York City government's police, fire, and emergency response agencies. They clearly saw that the positive impact on their future leaders was worth the time and expense.

Another concern about the 360-degree process is multiple raters may lead to discrepancies in feedback due to differing perspectives. Critics also suggest that the participants might choose people they believe are personally favorable or supportive, potentially skewing the feedback. From another perspective, there is a potential for an excessive focus on negative aspects of performance, as facilitators or managers might emphasize weaknesses rather than a balanced view of overall performance.[35] Still, the evaluations are averaged independently and are therefore anonymous to the person being evaluated. Professionals running the 360-degree processes are experts in helping the recipients understand the feedback and put it in perspective.

Feedback plays a crucial role in facilitating improvement. The 360-degree feedback system uniquely integrates the benefits of providing feedback with performance evaluation by allowing colleagues to offer anonymous praise or critiques. Over the past decade, 360-degree feedback has garnered considerable attention as a valuable tool. Its utilization has become widespread among organizations from all three sectors around the globe, and its popularity has steadily increased.

The *critical incident technique* was developed by John Flanagan.[36] During World War II, the critical incident technique was used to identify effective pilot performance. This method employs a systematic set of interview procedures to gather comprehensive data on individuals' direct observations of their own or others' behavior. In early research, Flanagan asked combat veterans to describe incidents that had a significant positive or negative impact on their missions. For instance, pilots were prompted to recall moments of combat when they faced disorientation or severe vertigo and to detail the sensory experiences—such as sights, sounds, or feelings—that led to these episodes. Flanagan then analyzed these narratives to identify essential components for effective task performance, which proved to be more precise and useful compared to the previously employed vague criteria for selection and training.

After the war, John Flanagan refined the system and applied it extensively across various industrial contexts. This technique helped establish ethical standards for psychologists, assess task proficiency, select and classify personnel, design job procedures and equipment, identify motivational and leadership attitudes, and determine factors contributing to effective counseling.[37]

The main advantage of the critical incident technique is also its most important limitation. Its primary strength lies in its focused examination of specific incidents that either facilitate or obstruct performance within experiences or activities. This precise focus allows for a detailed understanding of critical factors influencing effectiveness. However, the technique's concentration on specific incidents may lead to an overly narrow perspective, potentially overlooking broader contextual factors and general performance trends. Although it provides valuable insights into aspects of behavior and performance, its applicability may be constrained by its limited scope, which could affect its utility in capturing comprehensive, long-term patterns of performance and behavior.

Cultural and behavioral assessments analyze and manage organizational culture. They seek to define the culture with precision. Every organization inherently or explicitly adopts a competitive strategy that determines its positioning relative to competitors. Once this strategy is set, it prescribes a series of critical tasks or objectives that must be achieved through alignment among the components of people, structure, and culture.[38]

Organizational culture is frequently described as the fundamental force that integrates various aspects of an organization, often referred to as the "glue that holds organizations together."[39] It is not merely a component but rather the core of organizational dynamics, influencing all operational facets and playing a crucial role in the success of manufacturing strategies.[40] On a more detailed level, there is substantial evidence linking the alignment of employees with the organizational culture to important outcomes such as job commitment and turnover rates.[41]

To evaluate these cultural and behavioral dimensions, organizations typically use a range of methods. Surveys and questionnaires are often used to capture employees' perceptions of both organizational culture and their own behavior. In addition, interviews, focus groups, and observational techniques provide deeper insights into the nuances of culture and real-time behavioral interactions. Cultural and behavioral assessments are often understood as the psychological connection an individual has with an organization, encompassing aspects such as job involvement, loyalty, and alignment with organizational values.

Commitment to an organization typically progresses through three stages: compliance, identification, and internalization. In the compliance stage, individuals conform to the influence of others primarily to gain rewards, such as compensation. During the identification stage, individuals align themselves with the organization to maintain a fulfilling, self-defining relationship, deriving a sense of pride from their association with the organization. The final stage, internalization, occurs when individuals find the organization's values intrinsically rewarding and in harmony with their personal values.[42] Assessments of team climate and employee satisfaction are used to evaluate how well employees integrate into and fit within the work environment.

Despite significant interest in organizational culture, numerous questions remain unresolved regarding its definition and content, the methodologies for its measurement, and, more fundamentally, the practicality of managing and changing culture.[43] This is particularly the case when trying to match organizational culture with specific organizational objectives. Although these debates persist, organizational culture has been widely recognized by managers as a fundamental element of organizational life and has become a key component of numerous organizational development initiatives.

The three qualitative metrics offer distinct insights into organizational dynamics. The 360-degree feedback system provides a comprehensive view of performance by gathering evaluations from various sources, supporting self-development and strategic coherence, although it can be costly and biased. The critical incident technique focuses on detailed accounts of significant incidents affecting performance, providing deep insights into specific behaviors while potentially missing broader trends. Cultural and behavioral assessments examine how well employees fit with organizational culture through surveys and observations, shedding light on job involvement and satisfaction, but face challenges in precisely defining and measuring culture. Together, these methods offer complementary perspectives on organizational performance.

To be successful, organizations must ensure that their performance metrics not only focus on financial success but also address environmental stewardship, social equity, and long-term viability. Effective performance measurement systems balance traditional quantitative metrics with qualitative assessments to evaluate impacts across economic, environmental, and social dimensions.

CONCLUSION: PERFORMANCE MANAGEMENT CHECKLIST

We believe sustainable success for any organization is difficult, if not impossible, without the deployment of a robust and constantly refreshed performance management system. From a financial perspective, it is essential to prioritize long-term financial performance. Emphasizing short-term financial results can pressure managers to cut investments in crucial areas such as new product development, human resource development, process improvements, information technology, databases, and customer and market development. From the customer's perspective, core outcome measures should include customer satisfaction, customer profitability, customer retention, new customer acquisition, and market and account share in targeted segments.[44] This integrated approach supports the Sustainable Development Goals by promoting a holistic view of success that encompasses not just financial returns but also contributions to a more sustainable and equitable world.

Over many years of practice and study, we have identified ten key steps to effective and sustainable performance management systems:

1. Balance the number of KPIs. Having too few increases the danger of not measuring important indicators of success, but having too many confuses employees and stakeholders and diminishes the importance of each indicator.
2. Measure only what you will manage and hold people accountable.
3. Constantly search for potential danger in aspects of your operation for which there are no indicators.
4. Hold people and teams accountable for improvement and emphasize getting better. Inflated targets simply demoralize your teams and encourage data manipulation.
5. Make sure that each set of indicators has a stakeholder audience and that the audience for those indicators receives regular reports on the indicators.
6. Involve all sectors of the organization in the development of your indicators and in periodic reviews to add, subtract, and modify the measures used.
7. Focus on measuring and improving current levels of performance, but if targets must be set, analyze targets met, exceeded, and missed—you can learn from all three.
8. Seek a balance of input, process, output, and outcome/impact measures. Overall, for performance measurement and management, we have learned to focus more on outcomes rather than outputs.
9. Sustainability metrics are increasingly the most important measures to ensure both survival and impact.
10. Make sure you verify and audit all data and reports independently and regularly.

The next chapter introduces the concepts and practices of sustainability metrics and sustainability management. Sustainability management refers to the organizational practices needed to meet sustainability goals, whereas sustainability metrics involve tracking progress toward sustainability.

2

SUSTAINABILITY METRICS AND THE TRANSITION TO SUSTAINABILITY MANAGEMENT

This chapter defines sustainability metrics and sustainability management and distinguishes measures of environmental sustainability and measures of environment, social impact, and organizational governance (ESG). It analyzes the importance and complexity of measuring sustainability and the challenges of integrating sustainability metrics into sustainability management. We conclude by summarizing the macro trends that will influence the use of sustainability management as we transition to a renewable resource-based economy.

DEFINING SUSTAINABILITY METRICS

Many of the world's top corporations and nonprofits have been working to adopt sustainability measurement and management. Organizational managers are increasingly saving money while reducing the environmental damage caused by their organizations. Moreover, the best and brightest brains they hope to attract to work with them value the planet and want to ensure that the organizations they are building don't destroy it. Environmental protection is no longer a frill but a necessity for the modern corporation.

In 2020, *Wall Street Journal* reporters Dieter Holger and Fabiana Negrin Ochoa reported on the growth of corporate sustainability reporting. According to Holger and Ochoa:

> A new *Wall Street Journal* ranking of the world's most sustainably managed firms, underscores how sustainability reporting is capturing the corporate world. Not only are companies facing demands from some investors for data on their environmental, social, and governance (ESG) risks and practices, they are also being pressured by employees and consumers to focus on issues such as climate change and diversity. Last year, 90 percent of companies in the S&P 500 index published sustainability reports, up from about 20 percent in 2011, according to Governance & Accountability Institute, a New York-based consulting firm. As disclosure has improved, so has the value of corporate ESG data, researchers say. Assets under management in funds worldwide that weigh sustainability factors when making investment decisions grew to $40.5 trillion this year from $22.9 trillion in 2016.[1]

The increased prevalence of corporate sustainability reporting is a strong indicator of the importance of sustainability in twenty-first-century corporate management. Our private sector must compete on a more crowded, resource-challenged planet. Ideological politicians might be able to spin these issues and pretend they are not real for a short period of time, but corporate performance must operate in the actual world. A major problem with sustainability management and measurement, recognized by all concerned, is the different definitions assigned to the concept and the wildly different metrics utilized when measuring it. Central to the conceptual fuzziness has been the effort to create an index or ranking system that combines indicators of environmental sustainability with measures of a company's work to promote workplace fairness and equity as well as positive community impacts.[2] Our view is that this has been an effort to combine all the "do-gooder" elements of corporate behavior into a single measure. We do not see these practices as examples of corporate altruism but instead as evidence of effective management closely related to profit. Others act on the assumption that these are "add-ons" that do not contribute to corporate profit.[3] Although it can be more transparent and easy to understand for the public, the effort to measure these very different areas of performance in a single measure can overgeneralize. The organization's environmental performance and efforts to be good places to work and have a positive social impact are three separate concepts that should have three distinct sets of measures.

A second problem with sustainability measurement today is that dozens of nongovernmental organizations (NGOs) depend on the revenue they generate by analyzing and scoring corporate sustainability. This leads to an inherent conflict of interest in the current system of measurement.[4] Some measures focus on what we call environmental sustainability. Others, typically experts in human resource management, focus on workplace equity and fairness. Another field rooted in sociology or public policy study seeks to measure corporate impact on and engagement with local communities. Each of these elements of corporate performance should be measured and understood. However, these critical performance measures must be designed and regulated by the government. The model we favor is that we imitate the approach taken when we developed generally accepted accounting principles and require sustainability reporting by publicly owned corporations and audits by organizations certified by the government to conduct those audits.

We consider measures of environmental sustainability, measures of workplace equity, and measures of corporate community impact as distinct but routine measures of corporate performance. Our argument is that these measures are central to corporate performance and need to be understood by investors. An organization that pollutes, emits greenhouse gases, and wastes energy and other resources is an organization that is likely to be poorly managed in other ways and, in any case, is at risk of incurring damage charges due to environmental liabilities. An organization that treats its workers poorly poses risks to investors in an increasingly brain-based economy. An organization that neglects or damages its home communities will find its expansion constrained and its brand degraded. An example (and one we will mention frequently) is Amazon's failed attempt to locate a campus in Long Island City, New York.[5] Just as financial indicators provide compelling evidence of corporate performance, so too do these other indicators. Later in this book, we discuss the connection of sustainability indicators to performance indicators and the connection of all of these nonfinancial indicators to financial indicators.

In the case of environmental sustainability, we believe we need to develop a set of generally accepted environmental sustainability indicators. Measures of energy use, water use, material use, waste management/product reuse, pollution, and greenhouse gas emissions should be developed for service and manufacturing organizations. Just as financial indicators have been refined by the government over time, so too should these indicators. Sustainability units in corporations could be charged with reporting on these measures, and the NGOs and private firms now producing corporate sustainability reports could be trained and certified by the US federal government to audit these reports. Accounting firms engaged in corporate financial audits are already adding capacity to produce corporate sustainability reports. Standard indicators would be developed and reported. The same process could be repeated for workplace equity and community impact.

The unregulated sustainability measurement system now employed is reminiscent of US corporate financial reporting in the 1920s. The result back then was a stock market less reputable than a mob-run casino and the crash of 1929.[6] Investors had no real information on the value of their investments. The New Deal innovation of regulated corporate reporting under the Securities and Exchange Commission (SEC) helped correct that deficiency and eventually built a huge market for corporate securities.[7] This regulated financial reporting system contributed to the economic prosperity of the second half of the twentieth century. It provided investors with the confidence that their cash would be better off invested than stashed under their mattresses. A similar system could stimulate the corporate behaviors needed to reduce environmental damage, increase fairness and opportunity in human resource management, and reduce negative impacts on the communities that organizations operate within.

Corporate interest in sustainability measurement and reporting is a reflection of changes in environmental perceptions and values. It is an indicator of changes in the objective reality of life on this planet. People recognize that we must start applying our ingenuity and brainpower to the problem of supporting the material needs of a planet that will probably peak at a human population of ten billion.[8] If we are to have sustainable peace and prosperity on this planet, a fairer and more equitable set of national societies needs to develop.[9] Corporate behavior can have an enormous impact on our ability to achieve these goals. To influence corporate behavior, we need to integrate environmental performance into a company's ability to attract capital.

Environmental performance is not more important than issues of social governance, but it is easier to measure. A greenhouse gas emission and lead in drinking water are physical phenomena that can be easily measured. A company's impact on a community is measurable, but the measures are more difficult to develop and analyze. Nevertheless, as we often say in this book, in order to manage something, it needs to be measured. Without measurement, it is impossible to know if performance is getting better or worse. Although we do not think that it makes sense to measure ESG in a single indicator, we do believe these elements of organizational performance must be measured, and performance in these areas must be integrated into overall corporate management.

The specific sustainability measures used by each organization should strive for a common and generally accepted definition, but the measures and weight of each measure will differ by organization. An organization that manufactures clothing will utilize or at least weigh measures differently than a university or a software company. But a typical set of measures includes the physical, organizational, and community impact indicators found below in figure 2.1.

Contemporary corporate sustainability reporting, unlike financial reporting, tends to be unregulated and unaudited.[10] Regulation

1 Physical

- Water use
- Energy efficiency and source
- Waste production, disposal, and use
- Environmental impact on air, land, and water
    - Including but not limited to greenhouse gases
- Material use: Renewable, finite, and rare
- Land use: Impact on biodiversity and ecological well-being
- Climate risk: Impact of sea level rise and extreme weather on operations

2 Organizational

- Diversity of the lived experiences of staff, management, and participants in the governance structure
- Pay equity (not equality, but fairness)
- Staff perceptions of management
- Turnover rate
- Promotion potential and recruitment actions

3 Community

- Engagement activities
- Stakeholder perceptions of the organization
- Consumer/public perceptions of the organization

Figure 2.1 Summary of Key Sustainability Indicators

on the definition for these measures is increasingly important, and without such standards, their usefulness is limited for management, stakeholders, and investors. Until regulatory standards are in place, we believe it is essential that an organization's sustainability reporting be audited by an organization that is not dependent on the fees paid by the organization being audited. Therefore, the audit is paid for by the company, but the standards are not developed by the organization engaged in the audit but rather by the government.

DEFINING SUSTAINABILITY MANAGEMENT

Sustainability management can be defined as the organizational practices that foster environmental sustainability and organizational diversity, as well as minimal negative and maximal positive social and community impacts. The practices involve developing greater precision in undertaking organizational action and care in measuring and understanding the organization's impact on its surrounding community and the world.

The definition of sustainability management has evolved over the past decade and a half. In 2009, Steven Cohen was looking to combine environmental considerations with effective organizational management. As he examined the field of organizational management in the twenty-first century, he saw environmental issues becoming increasingly central to the field of management. This led to his 2010 book *Sustainability Management* and the development of Columbia's master of science program in sustainability management.[11] As the faculty designed the curriculum, they developed an area of management study called "the physical dimensions of sustainability management." This included energy efficiency, renewable energy, waste management, climate science, environmental science, ecology, toxicology, hydrology, green architecture, and other topics that had a physical or scientific component that managers needed to understand in addition to typical management topics such as finance, organizational management, strategy, marketing, quantitative analysis, financial and performance management, and human resource management.

In the decade-plus since then, Columbia faculty have broadened the field to include issues of diversity, equity, inclusion, corporate governance, and community impact, and the graduate degree now includes courses on forests, public space, the circular economy, corporate sustainability reporting, sustainable fashion, sustainability finance, and a variety of new and fascinating topics. Sustainability finance as a subfield now includes green accounting, energy finance, climate finance, financing the clean energy economy, energy markets and innovation, sustainable investing and economic growth, and impact finance. Another key addition to the discipline is the study of greenhouse gas measurement and sustainability metrics.

We acknowledge the political and ideological attack on sustainability management. Some political advocates question today's modern management practices where decision-makers factor in environmental impacts, promotion of diversity, issues of corporate governance, reporting of environmental risks, and community impact.[12] These same ideologues have also been aggressively promoting fossil fuels, even when the companies that use energy are resisting its use. They call consideration of environment and diversity "woke" capitalism and think that multidimensional and sophisticated sustainability management is some kind of left-wing plot.[13] This is unfortunate because, in our view, companies are trying to reduce their environmental risk and move toward renewable energy because they correctly believe it will enhance their profits. We are not arguing that all companies attempting to factor in ESG considerations are competent at doing so. There are also some overzealous ideologues promoting ESG principles. In our view, ESG management is misunderstood by ideologues of both the left and the right. Nevertheless, as with any new management practice, it takes a while to take hold and learn its limitations. Total Quality Management, team management, performance measurement and management, and numerous other new management practices (including accounting in the 1930s) have been gradually adjusted and included in organizational management.[14] As a result, modern corporations are nimbler and more productive than their predecessors in the mid-twentieth century. We believe that with ESG measures and carefully managed use of artificial intelligence, twenty-first-century organizations will become increasingly efficient and effective.

The carbon disclosure rules enacted by the European Union and California, the subsidies in the Inflation Reduction and Infrastructure Acts, and other local and international initiatives are already stimulating billions of dollars of investment in the transition to a modern, renewable resource-based economy. Like any technological and economic transition, these changes are poorly understood by many people and feared by those who believe their self-interest is threatened. When New York City lost its manufacturing base, many thought the city would die. Instead, it replaced that old economy with a brain-based service economy, perhaps best symbolized by the High Line, a freight train track transformed into a tourist attraction.[15] New York is a thriving city despite the pain of a generation-long economic transition. What we know about these transitions is that they are very difficult to stop. In a free-market, capitalist system, most of the incentives favor innovation and the rapid diffusion of new technologies. Often, these practices threaten environmental quality. We see that with the chemical industry, for example. However, the energy transition, which is well underway, will aim to utilize technology that will produce less air pollution and help mitigate global warming.

New technologies and more sophisticated management techniques are being developed constantly to help deal with our more complex, interdependent world economy. Innovative technologies enable this complex new world, and paradoxically, they are stimulated in part by the problems *created* by these new technologies. Scientists and engineers are hard at work improving solar cells. They are using nanotechnology to reduce their size and cost while increasing their efficiency.[16] Artificial intelligence and robotics are being used to enhance recycling and waste-mining and to reduce wasted fertilizer, pesticides, and water in agriculture.[17] Somewhere in the world, a couple of teenagers are working in a basement on a breakthrough that will radically improve battery technology. Even if they fail, some engineering faculty working with their students may succeed. Along with these engineering technologies, management experts and social scientists are learning more about how we can be more productive when we engage with each other in organizational settings. Data-driven management, enhanced employee rights, staff performance appraisal systems, and increased focus on turnover and morale are not random or rare occurrences. They are central elements of sophisticated, successful modern management. So, too, is consideration of the impact of the organization on its natural environment and surrounding community. Organizations that ignore the cost and environmental impact of their energy sources or favor existing sources out of fear or habit are likely to miss other opportunities to improve their performance.

Most American private and nonprofit organizations are embracing sustainability management, along with a wide variety of new production and management technologies. The search for improvement is continuous, and it is why our economy continues to innovate and produce. Economic and technological change has been proceeding since the dawn of civilization, but it has increased in speed over the past two centuries. Still, the pace is gradual and often invisible while it is underway. America's transition from a manufacturing to a service economy was invisible to many while it was advancing. A sustainable, renewable resource-based economy is both possible and necessary. It will require a process that will take decades to complete.

A careful, parsimonious approach to the use of physical materials that limits waste will make a production process more efficient and lower priced. We saw this when Total Quality Management reduced manufacturing waste and improved product quality in postwar Japan. In the 1950s and 1960s, "made in Japan" signified a low-quality product.[18] By the 1980s, Japanese automobiles and electronics had developed a reputation for high quality and high value.[19] As technology continues to develop, energy efficiency and renewable energy will beat other forms of energy on price, convenience, and efficiency. If we maintain a regulatory structure that punishes companies that release poison into the environment, the effort to reduce the risk of environmental liability will also result in cleaner production processes. Cities are being retrofitted for sustainability with sewage treatment and other infrastructure being designed to reduce our environmental impact.

In fact, our view of sustainability management is shaped by W. Edwards Deming's concepts of Total Quality Management.[20] To Deming, one of the functions of management was to free up workers to analyze and improve work processes with the goal of reducing waste and improving quality and customer satisfaction. Workers and management analyze how work is undertaken and seek to save time, labor, and material. Under this paradigm, pollution is a form of waste. An emission or effluent that is discharged into the environment is a wasted piece of material. For example, could that material have been used somehow? Heat vented into the atmosphere could have been retained and used to generate electricity. Moreover, the disposal of material waste is far from cost-free. An organization can't simply dump its garbage on the side of the road, and the cost of waste disposal is growing. Energy inefficiency is a form of waste. If one can produce a good or service with a dollar's worth of energy, why would they want to use twice as much energy as they need and spend two dollars instead of one? When Walmart puts a solar array on the roof of their store and cuts their electricity bill by 75 percent,[21] the green principle they are following looks more like a dollar than a tree.

Modern economic and social life has become less based on brawn than on brains. That means that potentially increased attention will be paid to growing our economy while reducing damage to the planet. The companies that mine minerals and manufacture material goods, like fossil fuel and steel companies, command far less economic power than companies like Google, Amazon, and Microsoft. Ultimately, this economic power will translate to political power, some of which will be devoted to ensuring free trade, immigration, and environmental protection—all policies that benefit these companies and their employees. The fossil fuel industry has an interest in burning oil; Amazon and Walmart need energy but have no reason to prefer fossil fuels to renewables. And based on all those solar arrays on the roofs of Walmarts, we suspect they've figured out the cost advantage of solar energy. The tariff, anti-immigration and antienvironmental, pro–fossil fuel policies pursued in both the first and second Trump administrations were quietly resisted by the giant service-based industries as they pursued their private interests and corporate profits. Global supply chains, talent drawn from the entire planet, and lower-priced energy benefit these companies, and regardless of ideological politicos, they continue to advance the practices that contribute to their success.

TRANSITIONING TO A RENEWABLE RESOURCE-BASED ECONOMY BUILT ON SUSTAINABLY MANAGED ORGANIZATIONS

There are at least six main stages in the transition to a renewable resource-based economy, and some will begin before others are completed. First, the theoretical or conceptual design of the transition must be fully articulated and understood. That phase is now underway. More and more people understand that we can't continue with a linear economy where every material we consume produces waste that ends up in a dump. The concept of a circular economy is becoming better known and understood. A circular economy, by definition, must be built on sustainably managed organizations. These organizations will rely on both traditional production metrics and the sustainability metrics that are the focus of this book.[22]

The second phase is to attract capital to the green economy. The SEC climate disclosure rule, which has been dropped by the second Trump administration, should *eventually* prevail because it's the job of the SEC to ensure corporate transparency for investors and increasingly investors are asking for reliable data on environmental risk.[23] Several NGOs have developed sustainability metrics, but this is too important an effort in governance to leave to the private for-profit or nonprofit sectors. Government must ensure that these metrics are developed and carefully audited when applied. We are already seeing the development of the field of sustainable investment. Over 90 percent of Standard and Poor's top 500 companies are issuing environment and social governance reports in 2025, and the size of green investments continues to grow.[24] These are all clear indications that this phase is underway. By the mid-2030s, we suspect this will be a mature element of the world of capital finance.

The third phase is the development of public capital for green infrastructure. The $1.2 trillion Biden infrastructure bill in 2021 included over $300 billion for public green investment—the largest single investment in environmental infrastructure in American history.[25] Although some of those funds were reduced by the second Trump administration, many funds were allocated and attracted private investment. Both California and New York have issued green bonds to provide capital for public green infrastructure investment.[26] This phase will take several decades to build momentum. The antitax and anti-investment ideology of the extreme right has been building momentum from the Reagan years to the Tea Party to the first and second Trump administrations. These days, we can't even raise the capital needed to repair bridges that are falling down, so green investments will need to be coupled with user fees whenever possible to retire debt. New York City's third water tunnel is an example of green infrastructure funded by water user fees. This water tunnel was built to enable the other two tunnels to be repaired over the next century, reducing water loss due to leakage. Infrastructure that directly generates revenues will be more readily constructed.

The fourth phase is the development of technology that supports an economy that grows without damaging the planet. This requires basic research funded by the government and tax credits and deductions for corporate research and development. There are a number of technologies we need to develop. Our current form of waste recycling is woefully inadequate. Home sorting of waste is a good educational exercise but little more. It is inefficient and often ineffective. We need to apply artificial intelligence and robotics to waste sorting and mining. Garbage must be a major source of resources in the future. We need to make food waste into fertilizer and mine garbage for plastics, metals, and all forms of material resources. We also need to improve and shrink solar cells with nanotechnology and improve battery capacity while reducing the toxicity of renewable energy technology. We need windows that serve as solar receptors and batteries the size of laptops that cost little and store solar and wind energy for periods without wind and sun. The current solar and battery technology beats fossil fuels in price but not performance.[27] The price needs to be way lower, and solar batteries need to work much better before they drive fossil fuels from the market. But all these technologies are coming. Although the attack on university-based science research in Trump 2.0 did not facilitate the development of these technologies, the need for these technologies provides the incentives for technological research and development to continue.

This fourth phase is well underway, and we are already seeing breakthroughs in new electric vehicle technologies. There have been breakthroughs in battery technology. Other improvements have been incremental. Think of cellphones and laptops at the turn of the twenty-first century and compare them to what we have today. It has been a slow but steady process of improvement.

The fifth phase is to develop the organizational capacity to utilize new technologies and seamlessly integrate the behaviors needed to produce goods and services with the least possible impact on the environment. This is well underway. Companies like Land O'Lakes are saving money by deploying agricultural practices that use as little water and chemicals as possible.[28] Drones and satellites, along with robotics and artificial intelligence, are lowering the cost and reducing the environmental impact of farming. Many organizations are building the capacity to minimize their carbon and environmental impacts. Key to this effort is developing and utilizing the sustainability metrics that enable organizations to institutionalize sustainability standard operating procedures.

Finally, the sixth phase is to build the organizational capacity, infrastructure, and capital needed to ensure widespread implementation, including retrofitting older facilities and elements of the built environment. This will be a gradual transition, taking at least a quarter-century to complete, although elements of the old economy will persist for many more years.

THE IMPORTANCE OF INTEGRATING SUSTAINABILITY METRICS INTO SUSTAINABILITY MANAGEMENT

The long-term trends and projections noted earlier will depend on sustainability metrics in sustainability management. This is discussed in detail in chapter 4, after a discussion of integrating sustainability measures into routine performance measurement systems and processes. We conclude this chapter, which provided a definition of sustainability metrics and sustainability management, by simply asserting that there can be no true sustainability management without sustainability metrics. Without practical and operational measures of an organization's sustainability, the concept is simply meaningless: symbolic at best and greenwashing at worst.

The use of nonsustainability performance indicators permeates organizational life, and nearly every organization manages operations against KPIs (Key Performance Indicators (KPIs). This provides an opening for sustainability metrics to simply be added to an organization's routine performance measurement system. Modern management depends on KPIs and, over time, closely relates KPIs to financial performance. We envision adding sustainability metrics to this existing organizational routine.

3

INTEGRATING SUSTAINABILITY METRICS INTO PERFORMANCE MEASUREMENT AND FINANCIAL PERFORMANCE

Performance measurement is the hallmark of modern management, and it is a process of determining whether progress is being made to achieve preset organizational goals and objectives. By definition, performance measurement collects data and analyzes it to track progress and evaluate how well the organization is performing toward its goals. Performance measurement is also important for benchmarking and comparing performances across organizations. We discussed the importance of performance measurement to the management of modern organizations in the first chapter of this book.

In the second chapter, we discussed the nature of sustainability metrics and elaborated on the use of metrics in sustainability management. In our view, sustainability management is the future of management and is the next phase in the long history of management innovation. Sustainability must be integrated into the heart of what organizations do—like international operations, information technology, mass production, financial management, and human resources were during the twentieth century. Organizations throughout the globe are attempting to reduce their carbon footprint, minimize climate and environmental risk, enhance resiliency, and incorporate sustainability into their operations.

The problem is they do not know how to do it. Companies, governments, and nonprofits are recognizing the need to take these actions, but their expertise lies in their own core functions, not in developing sustainability plans and assessing operational risk within this context. To take meaningful action on sustainability, corporations, nonprofits, and governments must bring sustainability into the regular fabric of organizational life. The physical dimensions of sustainability must now be added to standard operating procedures such that all managers become sustainability managers. Big ideas, ambitious goals, and beautiful policies don't translate into on-the-ground change until organizations change.

Therefore, in this chapter, we discuss the various approaches organizations can use to integrate sustainability metrics with conventional performance measurements. Specifically, this chapter offers an overview of various frameworks and methods for integrating these metrics, providing diverse approaches for organizations seeking to enhance their performance measurement systems. In addition, we address the obstacles organizations have faced in integrating sustainability metrics and whether the use of a multitude of indicators has improved management performance both internally and on the financial market.

THE THEORETICAL BASIS FOR INTEGRATING ENVIRONMENTAL, SOCIAL, AND GOVERNANCE (ESG) INFORMATION

Principal-agent theory holds that strong incentives can increase the risk of fraud. When there is asymmetric information—where principals, such as shareholders, cannot directly observe managerial effort—one solution is to link compensation to a broad range of success metrics, instead of only financial metrics.[1] This approach helps align interests and reduces the likelihood of managers acting solely in their own favor. By anchoring rewards to multiple indicators, the principal can better ensure that managerial actions align with broader organizational well-being, not only quarterly financial results, even in the face of information gaps.

A similar principle exists in decision theory, which asserts that combining diverse forecasts, whether from multiple analysts, experts, or models, can significantly improve accuracy.[2] This approach of averaging predictions to arrive at a more reliable estimate underpins many forecasting models across fields such as climate science, macroeconomic forecasting, energy demand projections, and even medical diagnosis. By integrating multiple perspectives, forecasters mitigate the impact of individual biases or errors, yielding more accurate outcomes overall. The multiple indicator approach to measurement is a central tenant of social science research methodology.

According to these theories, monitoring corporate performance should go beyond standard financial reports. In addition, it should include a diverse set of metrics known as nonfinancial performance indicators, including sustainability indicators. Incorporating these measures enables a fuller, more nuanced view of corporate health and resilience, helping investors and other stakeholders detect potential risks and opportunities that may not appear in financial statements alone.

One advantage of using multiple metrics is that it makes it more challenging to manipulate any single measure without detection. If a company were to artificially boost a high-stakes financial metric, such as earnings per share (EPS), the manipulated figure could appear out of sync with other disclosed nonfinancial indicators, revealing potential inconsistencies. This transparency can deter manipulation by increasing the likelihood that discrepancies will be detected.

Former US Supreme Court Justice Louis Brandeis famously noted that "sunlight is said to be the best of disinfectants; electric light the most efficient policeman."[3] His insight underscores the power of transparency to promote accountability and discourage misconduct. By shedding light on a wide array of performance indicators, investors can create an environment where management is less able to skew results for personal gain, thereby supporting a more honest and comprehensive approach to corporate oversight.

Second, financial statements have traditionally been designed to clarify a company's financial condition and provide investors with insights into its current monetary earnings. The origin of financial accounting is rooted in a system for safeguarding the interests of firm owners, and the discipline has long maintained a narrow focus on monetary transactions, considering only private costs and benefits. This focus becomes clear when contrasting the concepts of accounting profit and economic profit. Accounting profit is calculated as the monetary value of revenue generated by an entity minus the monetary expenses it incurs. Importantly, this measure of profit excludes the opportunity cost of capital—essentially, the value that could have been derived from alternate uses of financial, human, or natural capital. Economic profit, by contrast, considers the opportunity cost of both financial and human capital (although it still generally excludes natural capital), offering a broader perspective on profitability.[4]

Traditional financial accounting also ignores externalities—costs or benefits that affect an unrelated third party as a side effect of a transaction between two parties. This omission means that financial statements rarely capture the broader societal and environmental impacts of organizational activity. Yet, these impacts are increasingly relevant to stakeholders concerned with sustainability and the full social costs of an organization's operations. Accounting for externalities lies at the core of understanding the societal impact of organizational actions. Social and environmental accounting seeks to address these gaps by integrating concepts like full cost accounting to reflect the environmental and social effects of an organization's actions. This approach also provides a theoretical foundation for including ESG information in financial analysis, offering a more holistic view of organizational performance and sustainability.

The externality argument is similar to a principle in ESG that organizations need to be mindful of their impact on the local community. This is not a new concept; we see it when we compare the two banks in the classic Christmas movie *It's a Wonderful Life*. The Bailey Brothers Building and Loan is of and for the community, whereas Mr. Potter's bank was only in it for the money. As noted in chapter 2, in New York, a tone-deaf Amazon.com was unable to site its HQ2 in Long Island City when community leaders rebelled against a multi-billion-dollar subsidy for one of the world's richest companies.

In addition to these theoretical arguments, pollution is also a form of waste, and if one applies the principles of Total Quality Management and industrial ecology to production processes, a central goal is to reduce waste in order to reduce cost. In the case of pollution—or waste that impacts an organization's neighbors—cost can also include liability incurred by damaging someone else's property. These liability costs can extend to an organization's supply chain as well. Even if waste is safely disposed of, the cost of waste transport and disposal is real and growing.

Being careless about an organization's environmental impact is an indicator of inadequate management. Just as a construction project riddled with injuries and death is an indication of a poorly run operation, any operation that creates unnecessary risk from pollution indicates poor management. Under macho management, pollution-belching smokestacks are a sign of industrial might. In this approach, charging ahead without worrying about impact is a sign of strength: "In order to make an omelet, you have to break some eggs." The concept of "breakage" is baked into financial control systems and is assumed to be a routine cost of business. Under environmental sustainability management, precision, control, and care replace the sloppy habits of the early industrial era. The petrochemical companies in Louisiana's "Cancer Alley" continue to emit heat and poisons into the air and effluents in the water. At some point, their competitors will apply the techniques of industrial ecology to petrochemical manufacturing and find a way to contain these discharges and make money off of what once was considered waste. The "E" in ESG is about environmental care and concern.

INTEGRATING SUSTAINABILITY METRICS INTO PERFORMANCE MEASUREMENT

As sustainability becomes a critical aspect of corporate strategy, organizations are increasingly expected to measure and disclose their environmental, social, and governance impacts alongside traditional financial metrics. This holistic approach allows organizations to provide a balanced view of their performance, focusing not only on financial outcomes but also on societal and ecological impacts. Many frameworks and standards have emerged to facilitate the integration of sustainability indicators with traditional performance measurements. This section provides an overview of the main approaches to integrating such sustainability indicators, along with their benefits and challenges.

Historically, performance measurement systems were solely based on financial measures, such as revenue growth, profitability, market share, and return on investment. These measures were chiefly designed to estimate and predict the economic value created for shareholders. Later on, as we indicated earlier, nonfinancial performance indicators, such as organizational work processes, outputs, and outcomes, were added and also became key performance indicators. More recently, as the world has become more aware of environmental and social issues, many of the limitations of using solely financial and even internal production measures are being exposed. Traditional measures do not take into account the wider social and environmental impacts of business operations, including resource depletion, emissions, and labor practices, which can seriously affect cost, profitability, and reputation of a company. The financial and some operational indicators also poorly capture the risks related to environmental degradation and extreme weather events such as droughts, wildfires, flooding, and hurricanes. Although some argue that direct causal links between these types of events and climate change are not proven, it is clear that their intensity and frequency are increasing and organizations have to cope with them.

Therefore, the transition toward performance measurement that focuses on broader sustainability aims to adopt metrics representing the impact of an organization on natural, human, and social capital. This transition reflects a shift from a focus on internal operations and short-term gains in company financials to long-term value creation and risk management. By combining sustainability metrics with traditional financial and performance indicators, an organization can align its goals with the demands of diverse stakeholders as well as regulatory requirements. We next outline some of the well-known frameworks for integrating sustainability metrics.

The Triple Bottom Line Approach

The Triple Bottom Line (TBL) approach is the foundational model for integrating sustainability into performance measurement. It expands the traditional concept of "the bottom line" to encompass three interconnected dimensions: people (social impact), planet (environmental impact), and profit (financial impact).[5] This framework encourages organizations to consider the broader consequences of their operations, recognizing that long-term success depends on maintaining a balance between economic progress, societal well-being, and environmental sustainability.

In the social dimension, the TBL framework assesses a company's influence on its employees, communities, and society. Metrics in this area may include employee health and safety, diversity and inclusion, labor relations, community engagement, and adherence to human rights standards. Such social considerations are particularly significant in industries where labor relations and community involvement are important, such as in mining, agriculture, manufacturing, and retail, where a company's social performance can directly impact its reputation. There indicators are not equally important across all organizations, and each organization must adjust the framework to fit their own organizational functions and environment.

The social dimension is particularly important also in the context of global supply chains, where the social impact of business operations extends across diverse regions and communities. In global supply chains, where production and sourcing often involve multiple countries with varying labor standards and regulations, addressing the social aspect can be challenging but crucial for satisfying demands of local communities. Our Research Program on Sustainability Policy and Management at the Columbia Climate School once partnered with the Institute for Sustainable Communities on the evaluation of environment, health, and safety (EHS) training of supply chain employees for big clothing and shoe brands. We found that although the EHS training offered necessary skills and information to middle managers who were trained to become change agents to lead reduction in EHS problems and risks, they often lacked the drive and skills that could be turned into practice when they returned to the factory floor.[6]

The environmental dimension addresses a company's impact on the natural environment, evaluating its resource use and the contribution of company activities to environmental degradation. Commonly used metrics in this area include carbon emissions, energy consumption, waste generation, toxic releases, water usage, and biodiversity protection. Although these metrics are becoming relevant for companies across all sectors, they are especially important for sectors with significant environmental footprints, such as mining, manufacturing, energy, and transportation, where the pressure to reduce environmental impact is particularly high due to regulatory requirements and stakeholder expectations.

Finally, while the financial dimension still focuses on traditional metrics such as revenue, cost, and profitability, it can also integrates financial values created from sustainability initiatives. For instance, with the sustainability transition in mind, companies now measure the cost savings from energy efficiency and recycling programs, the financial gains from newly developed sustainable product lines, and possible economic benefits of improved labor practices. The monetization of sustainability initiatives allows companies to better understand the relationship between their sustainability efforts and financial performance.

There are also some well-known challenges associated with implementing a TBL approach. As we have previously discussed, social and environmental metrics often lack consistency across industries, and the qualitative nature of many social metrics can introduce subjectivity, making it difficult to achieve uniform benchmarks or standardize across metrics. Additionally, when we introduce additional sustainability objectives, companies may face competing objectives, especially in situations where immediate financial returns do not align with long-term sustainability goals. Many of the following frameworks build on the TBL concept. To successfully adopt the TBL framework, companies have to overcome these problems by designing targeted metrics, aligning short-term financial objectives with long-term goals such as adapting to climate risks, and show a willingness to address employee and community concerns.

The United Nations Sustainable Development Goals

The Sustainable Development Goals (SDGs) are a well-known set of seventeen global objectives designed by the United Nations (UN). They aim to address a wide range of social, economic, and environmental challenges in an equitable manner by 2030. The goals were adopted by all UN member states in 2015 and constitute part of the 2030 Agenda for Sustainable Development.[7]

The development of the SDGs began with the need to replace the Millennium Development Goals (MDGs), which were established in 2000 and set targets for reducing poverty, hunger, and disease by 2015. Although the MDGs made some progress in areas of poverty reduction, especially in countries like India and China, they were criticized for being narrow in scope and focused only on developing countries. In addition, the MDGs did not focus on environmental sustainability or inequity, which are shared objectives of all countries regardless of their stages of economic development. Subsequently, the process of creating the SDGs was much more inclusive and involved extensive consultations with governments, civil society, businesses, and citizens worldwide to ensure the goals reflected diverse global priorities. The United Nations Conference on Sustainable Development (Rio+20) in 2012 agreed to develop a new set of goals that would be universally applied to developed and developing countries alike, not only addressing poverty and social issues as highlighted in the MDGs but also incorporating environmental considerations, as well as two additional pillars in peace and partnerships, in a so-called 5P framework (people, planet, prosperity, peace, and partnership).

The SDGs are significant because they set a comprehensive global framework that encourages all countries to work together toward common goals. Unlike the MDGs, which focused on transfers of funds and technology from developed countries to reduce poverty in developing countries, the SDGs apply universally to all nations. Whereas the MDGs focused on governments, the SDGs emphasize collaboration among a diverse set of stakeholders, especially highlighting the important role played by businesses, many of which are larger financially than some nations.

Specifically for companies, the United Nations Global Compact, the Global Reporting Initiative, and the World Business Council for Sustainable Development jointly developed the SDG Compass to guide organizations in integrating the SDGs into their business strategy and measuring their contribution toward sustainable development. Using the SDG Compass, companies can align their strategic goals with the SDGs, set concrete targets, and report on their progress.[8] We present examples of how SDG Compass is used in practice by companies in chapter 5.

Integrating the SDGs into corporate strategies allows companies to measure their impact and progress against internationally recognized benchmarks. The SDG Compass is an example of how an organization can adopt the SDGs through a structured methodology of embedding sustainability into their core operations. Nowadays, most of the companies that publish sustainability-related reports have developed key performance indicators that match up to the SDGs and their underlying targets and indicators.

Despite its global support, achieving the SDGs presents many challenges. Political polarization is increasing around the world, making partnerships and collaborations more difficult. Environmental and resource limitations are increasing as well. The impact of global crises such as climate change and pandemics also makes it difficult to focus resources on poverty alleviation and achieving many of SDGs' social targets. In addition, although the SDGs provide a useful framework for companies to transition toward sustainability, there are significant challenges in integrating the SDG targets into business strategies, such as the difficulties associated with measuring impact, identifying goals that are most material to corporate businesses, and aligning short-term financial goals with long-term sustainability objectives.

The Global Reporting Initiative

The Global Reporting Initiative (GRI) framework is probably the most prominent adaptation of the TBL approach. Founded in 1997 by the Coalition for Environmentally Responsible Economies (CERES), the United Nations Environmental Program, and the Tellus Institute, the main objective of the GRI is to develop an internationally acceptable standard for nonfinancial reporting that allows organizations to disclose their impacts on a wide range of sustainability issues from human rights and labor practices to environmental management and governance. Because of its broad scope and TBL approach, the GRI framework is useful to organizations seeking to align their sustainability reporting with international benchmarks, such as the UN SDGs. The GRI also contains a set of universal standards, last updated in 2021, that should be used by all organizations who report through GRI. In addition to their universal standards, GRI also publishes forty sector-specific standards, such as coal, oil and gas, mining, and financial services, starting with the ones with the highest impact.[9] The sector standards are also updated regularly. These high-impact sector standards, as well as recently published topic standards that focus on specific issues such as climate change, allow companies to map their contributions to the SDGs, for example, SDG 13 on Climate Actions.

The multitude of nonfinancial indicators contained in the GRI framework ensures a multistakeholder approach, which encourages organizations to consider the interests and concerns of all their stakeholders, not just the interests of shareholders and investors. The stakeholder perspective acknowledges the fact that organizations have a responsibility to various constituencies, such as employees, customers, suppliers, and local communities, as well as to society at large.[10] GRI is by far the most prevalent framework used in sustainability reporting around the world.

Although GRI's comprehensive approach offers a more inclusive view of sustainability, it can also be very demanding in terms of data collection and reporting efforts. Organizations may need to gather extensive information across a wide range of topics, which can be resource intensive, a common problem with sustainability reporting. This is why many small and medium-sized companies, which are more cost-conscious compared to their larger counterparts, have been reluctant to implement sustainability in their organizations. Additionally, because the GRI framework is stakeholder oriented, it may not be favored by investors, who may prioritize sustainability data that is only financially relevant.

Integrated Reporting

Integrated Reporting (IR) is another well-known sustainability framework, but unlike GRI, which is stakeholder focused, IR is more applicable to investors. It was developed by the International Integrated Reporting Council (IIRC), a global coalition of regulators, investors, companies, standard setters, the accounting profession, and nongovernmental organizations (NGOs). IR seeks to merge financial and nonfinancial metrics into a single cohesive report. IR follows a "multicapital" approach to provide investors with a comprehensive understanding of how an organization creates value over time by considering not only returns to financial capital but also other forms of capital, including manufactured, intellectual, human, social and relationship, and natural capital.[11] Similar to other sustainability frameworks, IR also aims to go beyond the traditional scope of financial statements and capture a range of nonfinancial capital that can contribute to a company's long-term success.

As outlined in the IIRC report, the concept of "capital" within IR is broader than the financial capital measured by conventional accounting. Manufactured capital, for instance, includes physical infrastructure and technology used in production, whereas intellectual capital encompasses organizational knowledge and innovation potential. Human capital is concerned with employee skills, engagement, and well-being, and social and relationship capital reflects the company's connections with customers, suppliers, and the broader community. Natural capital, on the other hand, considers the organization's use of environmental resources and its impact on ecosystem services. However, unlike the GRI, which focuses on diverse stakeholders, the IR framework explicitly targets providers of financial capital while also recognizing the importance of the other forms of capital.

Traditional economic modeling only considers financial capital and treats other forms of capital as externalities. The IR approach takes into account the enormous value created from the other forms of capital. This provides a more holistic view of value creation, guiding stakeholders to understand the interplay between different types of resources and their impact on financial performance. For example, investments in employee training (human capital) can enhance innovation (intellectual capital), which, in turn, contributes to better financial results. Because of the interconnectedness of capital, the metrics are also interconnected, linking financial performance to sustainability outcomes. For example, there are cost-saving metrics from energy efficiency or improved recycling, as well as metrics of brand value improvement from responsible sourcing.

However, the transition to IR can be demanding. IR is significantly more difficult to adopt than the GRI framework because one needs to reevaluate the business model and how it creates value using the previously outlined six forms of capital. As a result, the IR framework is more widely adopted than the GRI in South Africa, where the Johannesburg Stock Exchange had required IR for its publicly listed companies, as well as in the United Kingdom and some Scandinavian countries like Sweden and Denmark for their private and public companies.

A central problem with IR is its system for grading corporations on a single composite rating metric. The grading system encourages companies that have no impact on a variety of graded factors to issue symbolic and meaningless statements to demonstrate adherence to principles that have nothing to do with corporate functioning. For example, a service-oriented firm in the United States gets points for issuing a human rights policy and articulating their opposition to forced labor. They also get points for issuing a public ESG report, regardless of substance. This process orientation and effort to hold widely different organizations to a single composite indicator demonstrate a problem we previewed in earlier chapters.

Sustainability Accounting Standards Board

In contrast with the GRI framework, which is much more comprehensive and stakeholder centric, the framework developed by the Sustainability Accounting Standards Board (SASB) in the United States is focused on investors, similar to the IR framework developed by IIRC. These two investor-centric organizations merged in 2021, a development that simplified the corporate sustainability reporting landscape.

Organizations can still use the SASB framework, which is the most investor-focused sustainability framework available, and it provides a set of standards for companies to disclose financially material sustainability information under five broad dimensions: environment, human capital, social capital, business model and innovation, and leadership and governance. The standards are industry specific, recognizing that sustainability issues impact different sectors differently. For example, the risks from climate change may be more significant for energy companies, and the concerns about data privacy may be more relevant to the technology sector. In addressing these disparities, SASB has developed standards for seventy-nine industries, covering ESG topics that are most likely to financially impact organizations from different sectors.[12]

The SASB framework primarily focuses on financial materiality, which highlights the financial impacts of sustainability factors. It has also developed an SASB Materiality Map to guide companies in their assessment of materiality by sector and sustainability issue.[13] The distinction of materiality by sector is significant because, for example, carbon emissions are more material for the transportation sector than the financial sector, whereas business ethics may well be more material for the healthcare sector than the communication sector. However, one of the challenges with SASB's investor-centric approach is that it emphasizes financially material issues, which may not capture all the sustainability topics that stakeholders such as employees, customers, or communities might consider important.

The Balanced Scorecard with Sustainability Indicators

As mentioned in chapter 1, the balanced scorecard is a performance management tool developed by Robert Kaplan and David Norton in 1996.[14] It evaluates organizational performance through four perspectives: financial, customer, internal processes, and learning and growth. When integrating sustainability metrics, companies can embed relevant environmental and social indicators within these perspectives, thereby expanding the scorecard to reflect broader strategic goals. Similar to the other frameworks we have already outlined, sustainability indicators may be incorporated into the financial perspective through metrics such as cost savings from resource efficiency or revenue generated from sustainable products. The customer perspective may capture customer satisfaction–related measures of corporate social responsibility initiatives or market share of sustainable products. The perspective when we focus on internal processes can enable us to monitor improvements in energy efficiency, waste reduction, or adoption of renewable energy sources. The learning and growth perspective may include metrics for employee training in sustainability practices, progress toward meeting diversity targets, and corporate culture that supports sustainability.

The balanced scorecard approach helps organizations integrate sustainability goals with their strategic priorities so that the sustainability initiatives become part of regular operations and the decision-making process within the organization. However, integration of sustainability measures into the traditional balanced scorecard requires careful evaluation of the most relevant indicators with respect to the organizational objectives and constant efforts to modify and improve the scorecard because sustainability priorities may evolve over time.

In addition, the development of a *sustainable* balanced scorecard extends the traditional balanced scorecard by explicitly incorporating sustainability objectives into strategic performance measurement. In addition to adding sustainability indicators to the traditional scorecard perspectives as outlined earlier, companies may choose to add sustainability-specific perspectives to a sustainable balanced scorecard, such as environmental stewardship or social responsibility.[15] The sustainable balanced scorecard allows companies to embed sustainability directly into their strategic planning, hence ensuring that sustainability considerations are prioritized throughout the organization. However, adapting the scorecard to address specific sustainability issues may require significant customization and effort, particularly for industries with diverse sustainability challenges.[16]

Value-Based Management Enhanced with ESG Factors

The frameworks outlined above can be utilized by organization managers to implement and report on sustainability. The Value-Based Management (VBM) approach focuses on maximizing shareholder value by linking management practices directly to financial outcomes. By incorporating ESG factors into VBM, companies can better assess how sustainability-related risks and opportunities impact their financial valuation. Adjusting valuation models, such as discounted cash flow or economic value added, to account for ESG considerations allows organizations to understand how factors such as regulatory risks associated with carbon emissions or the financial benefits of sustainable labor practices influence long-term value creation.[17]

For example, incorporating potential regulatory changes related to carbon emissions into a discounted cash flow model can provide insights into future financial risks or savings. Considering the economic value of social capital improvements—such as lower employee turnover or enhanced customer loyalty—can highlight the financial benefits of sustainability efforts. Despite its advantages, integrating ESG factors into VBM requires robust data on nonfinancial elements and may face challenges due to inconsistent ESG data quality and availability, as previously discussed.

Social Return on Investment

Similar to the VBM framework, the Social Return on Investment (SROI) framework also tries to monetize an organization's social and environmental activities. As its name suggests, instead of the traditional return on investment approach, which focuses solely on financial gains, the SROI accounts for broader societal impacts, enabling organizations to demonstrate the value they generate or mitigate through their initiatives. The calculation of SROI involves several steps: establishing scope and stakeholders, mapping outcomes, assigning monetary values to those outcomes, assessing actual impact by considering factors such as deadweight and attribution, calculating the SROI ratio (total social value divided by total investment), and reporting the results.[18]

SROI provides a more holistic evaluation of value creation by including societal impact, which is useful to broader stakeholders. However, the approach also faces challenges, such as the difficulty associated with monetizing intangible outcomes, potential subjectivity in using financial proxies, and the limitations of focusing on quantifiable results.[19] For instance, monetizing the benefit from improved mental health or community cohesion may be difficult because they lack agreed-upon monetary values. Moreover, using financial proxies, such as future earning potential, can be arbitrary and may not always reflect the different circumstances of the beneficiaries. Conversely, focusing solely on measurable outputs, such as employment rates, overlooks qualitative benefits, which can include increased self-esteem and social skills. Another related consideration is stakeholder variability: whereas local residents may celebrate lower-cost housing, businesses might complain about traffic congestion. Finally, establishing the precise contribution made by an intervention can be difficult if simultaneous programs are leading to similar outcomes, compounding the overall assessment of the SROI. We should also note that these are challenges not only confined to the SROI but also more broadly related to how we monetize ESG. Although not without limitations, SROI remains a valuable tool for understanding and integrating social impact with financial impact.

Natural Capital Accounting

Similar to SROI, natural capital accounting is also a framework that aims to quantify the financial impact of nonfinancial factors. However, the focus is now on measuring and quantifying the value of natural resources and ecosystems in monetary terms. Natural capital accounting uses ecological and economic parameters to assess the contribution of nature to human well-being and economic progress. By accounting for natural capital in addition to financial and manufactured capital, organizations and governments can better appreciate the value of ecosystem services—such as clean air, water, biodiversity, and carbon sequestration—and incorporate these values into their decision-making processes.

Natural capital accounting first identifies the stocks and flows of natural resources. It then monetizes their value by estimating the benefits we derive from ecosystems as well as the potential costs associated with their degradation.[20] The accounting process utilizes a number of valuation methods, including contingent valuation, cost-benefit analysis, and ecosystem service assessments, to assign monetary values to natural assets.[21] This approach of accounting for the value of natural capital highlights the economic implications of environmental degradation and allows policymakers and businesses to recognize the trade-offs between development and conservation, and can help us overcome some of the problems we have identified with monetizing ESG indicators.

In addition, including natural capital in national accounts allows government agencies to enact policies that encourage practices and investments that protect and enhance ecosystem health. More broadly, natural capital accounting can demonstrate how natural resources contribute to economic growth and resilience, leading to better-informed policy choices and sustainable development. This methodology highlights the importance of preserving natural capital in ensuring the long-term viability of economies and the well-being of future generations. Therefore, natural capital accounting can be a very useful tool for promoting environmental sustainability and addressing global challenges like climate change and biodiversity loss, not just for organizations but also for countries.

Life Cycle Assessment

Life cycle assessment (LCA) provides a comprehensive overview of the environmental and financial impacts associated with products, services, or processes throughout their entire life cycles. It is a systematic process for assessing the environmental impacts at the product level, from raw material extraction through production, use, and disposal. Sometimes, it's referred to as a cradle-to-grave assessment. It starts with defining the goal and scope of the assessment, including system boundaries and the functional unit of measurement, and then moves on to the collection of data on inputs, such as energy, water, and materials, and outputs, such as emissions and waste. After inventory analysis, the next stage of LCA involves an evaluation of potential environmental impacts, such as greenhouse gas emissions and resource depletion, to understand the impact or "contributions" of the different life cycle stages. The final step is interpretation, where the results are analyzed to identify significant environmental impacts and areas for improvement.[22]

It is common practice now when calculating emissions of a product to include its use phase, along with the emissions generated during the extraction of material, construction, and disposal. In this way, LCA can help organizations optimize their product design and supply chain management by implementing higher sustainability and emission standards for their products and supplier companies.

Other Sustainability and Climate-Related Frameworks

The frameworks outlined in this book are by no means exhaustive. Although the GRI, SASB, and IIRC IR frameworks are intended for large corporations, frameworks such as the one developed by the

Impact Reporting and Investment Standards (IRIS) and B Impact are tailored for small and medium-sized enterprises.

Driven by the campus antiapartheid and environmental movements of the 1970s and 1980s, "impact investing" has transformed the public debate on economic growth. Defined by the Global Impact Investing Network (GIIN) as investments made "with the intention to generate positive, measurable social and environmental impact alongside a financial return," the impact investing market now is measured at more than a trillion dollars.[23]

As socially minded investment gained momentum in the 1990s, the Rockefeller Foundation began to reconsider its philanthropic investment strategies. "There was a recognition that philanthropy needed not only to do traditional grant making but to start thinking about mission-related investing," said Judith Rodin of the Rockefeller Foundation. This broader agenda, Rodin said, meant "not only not doing something"—like divesting from companies doing business in South Africa—but also "doing something that was proactive and positive."[24]

In her position, Rodin convened a group of bankers and other investors to explore the possibility of investments with a "double bottom line," which would measure not only financial gains but also social and environmental benefits from investments. In 2007, the Rockefeller Foundation convened a meeting at its conference center in Bellagio, Italy, and participants at that meeting coined the term "impact investing."[25]

The Rockefeller Foundation commissioned the Monitor Institute to write a report for the emerging practice. The resulting blueprint, published in 2009, identified four goals: creation of a common platform for investment, which led to the founding of GIIN; establishment of clear metrics, which emerged in the form of IRIS and the Global Impact Investing Rating System (GIIRS); creation of a process for working with companies, which was accomplished through funding B Lab and developed the B Corp Certification; and influencing public policy, including regulations such as the Employee Retirement Income Security Act (ERISA) in the United States, which mandate fiduciary duties that can act as an obstacle to impact investing.[26] The IRIS framework includes a list of metrics impact funds use to measure the environmental, social, and financial performances of their investee companies or projects, which tend to be small companies or community enterprises, whereas the B Impact framework is used as the basis by B Lab to certify B Corporations.

There are also well-known climate-related frameworks, such as the Climate Disclosure Standards Board (CDSB), the Carbon Disclosure Protocol (CDP), and the Task Force on Climate-Related Financial Disclosure (TCFD). The CDSB is an international consortium of business and environmental organizations that sets standards to improve the reporting of climate-related information and integrate them with existing financial reporting standards to help businesses communicate their climate-related risks, opportunities, and performance. The CDP is a global nonprofit organization that enables companies and cities to disclose their environmental impact, particularly related to carbon emissions and climate change risks and opportunities. Established by the Financial Stability Board, the TCFD also provides a framework for companies to disclose climate-related financial risks and opportunities. Its recommendations encourage organizations to assess and report on the impacts of climate change on their business strategy, governance, risk management, and performance. We will elaborate on some of these climate-related frameworks in chapter 6.

In addition to the frameworks that aim to quantify various sustainability or climate factors, there are various frameworks that have been established to qualitatively assess a range of composite environmental, social, and economic indicators. One such example is the Barometer of Sustainability, created by Robert Prescott-Allen in 1995,[27] which simultaneously evaluates both the environmental and social dimensions of sustainability. Another framework, the Eco-Efficiency Framework, first described by Stephan Schmidheiny and Federico Zorraquin in 1996,[28] was developed by the World Business Council on Sustainable Development (WBCSD) to help large corporations optimize their use of environmental resources, particularly in developing countries. Additionally, the Ecological Footprint developed by Wathis Wackernagel and William Rees in

1998[29] calculates the hypothetical area of land required to provide sufficient food, water, and energy, as well as to manage waste for an individual, product, or city.

The incredibly wide range of indicators and frameworks, although useful, can also be a source of friction, and the fragmentated requirements and expectations can be costly for firms when they have to use different disclosure frameworks to report to different rating agencies. In our view, this is indicative of the need for significant collaborations among different framework developers and standard setters to simplify the disclosure process. In the long run, we will need government to play a larger role in developing and refining measures and mandatory reporting requirements. This would emulate the practice of financial accounting, which is largely driven by government regulations observed to gain access to public financial markets. This sacrifices comprehensiveness for simplicity and enables organizations to structure tasks to enhance performance on these measures. In chapter 6, we discuss in greater detail the effort to achieve simplification after we review some of the climate-related frameworks.

Best Practices for Integrating Sustainability with Performance Measurement

Integrating sustainability with performance measurement involves adopting the best practices that can enhance organizational decision-making and drive sustainable outcomes. Below are some common steps:

- Establish a clear sustainability strategy. Align the sustainability strategy with organizational goals to ensure sustainability metrics are integrated into overall performance objectives. This alignment helps to create a unified vision and corporate culture, which can reinforce the importance of sustainability across the organization.
- Adopt a multistakeholder approach in selecting indicators. Always engage various stakeholders—employees, customers, suppliers, investors, academics, and community members—in identifying the most

relevant sustainability metrics. An inclusive process in identifying the metrics not only ensures that the selected indicators reflect diverse perspectives but also fosters a sense of ownership and shared commitment among stakeholders.

- Build sustainability data management systems. Develop robust data management systems to periodically collect, track, and report on sustainability performance information. Utilize both qualitative and quantitative metrics to capture the full range of sustainability impacts, from community responsibilities to environmental compliance and even biodiversity.
- Update the system on a regular basis. Regularly review and update sustainability metrics to reflect new research, evolving corporate objectives, changing regulatory environment, and stakeholder feedback. In some of the metrics systems that we have developed at Columbia for governments and companies, the indicators and weighting methodologies are usually adjusted every three to five years in order to respond to new and emerging sustainability challenges.
- Communicate effectively. Share sustainability performance outcomes with stakeholders and the broader public on a consistent basis to increase transparency and accountability. Openly communicate successes and challenges, and disclose future goals and targets. The publication of annual sustainability or ESG reports can help build trust and increase credibility.

SUSTAINABILITY METRICS AND FINANCIAL PERFORMANCE

The relationship between sustainability factors and corporate financial performance is of growing interest to companies and investors. As outlined in this chapter and elsewhere in this book, sustainability metrics can provide insight into whether a company will be able to manage risks (including nonfinancial risks) properly, use its resources efficiently, and develop long-term, sustainable strategies for growth. They go beyond mere indicators of environmental protection or charitable efforts and begin to define a company's fiscal trajectory by influencing its cost structure, risk profile, and investor perceptions.

Theory

Companies that perform well on sustainability metrics are generally viewed as better managers of resource constraints and potential risks, which can theoretically lead to better financial performance. In industries where natural resources are a critical part of business operations—such as in energy, mining, or agriculture—high environmental scores may reflect a company's forward-looking approach to managing environmental risks, improving regulatory compliance, and optimizing resource use. Specifically, sound sustainability practices can potentially help companies lower compliance and operational costs while at the same time making the companies more resilient and able to maintain long-term growth. These benefits are valuable for investors. For example, strong sustainability practices may signal to investors that a firm is less likely to be fined for environmental damage or suffer social backlash and hence is a safer investment. This is particularly relevant in industries that face stringent regulatory standards, where compliance can significantly affect financial stability.

In addition, companies adhering to sustainable practices often cut direct costs by way of waste reduction, recycling, energy efficiency, or improved labor practices. Good governance practices such as diverse, independent boards or clear ethical guidelines can help a company avoid misconduct, reduce employee turnover, and reduce potential legal liabilities. Over time, these improvements and cost reductions may translate into higher profitability, higher returns on equity, and even better stock performance. Perhaps more importantly, many hope that superior sustainability performance can lead to lower cost of capital, as a high sustainability rating might suggest lower perceived risk, which leads to lower borrowing costs and better access to capital.

Furthermore, there are divergent expectations for sustainability returns across different industries. In industries where regulatory risks, carbon liabilities, and social licensing are salient drivers, sustainability may lead to strong financial results, whereas the same initiatives may have only small impact in other industries. For instance, environmental issues are very important for utility companies, whereas governance issues are more important in finance or technology, where ethical business practices and compliance are critical.

Investor perspectives also play a key role in determining the relationship between sustainability and financial performance of companies. For long-term investors, companies that prioritize sustainability are seen as less risky and better positioned to weather regulatory or market changes in the long run, and organizations can justify the short-term costs associated with sustainability initiatives as necessary to ensure long-term growth and stability. In contrast, short-term investors may perceive the costs associated with implementing sustainability initiatives as a potential downside to financial performance, especially if these investments do not produce immediate financial gains.

Empirical Evidence

There is a large body of literature that explores the relationship between sustainability practices and financial performance. Studies have examined how various sustainability metrics are related to financial indicators like earnings per share (EPS), stock price, sales, profitability, and profit margins. At the same time, the universe of sustainability indicators has expanded significantly, covering everything from carbon footprint and waste management to employee welfare and corporate governance practices. However, *current research in economics and finance has yet to establish a definitive causal relationship between sustainability performance and consistently higher market returns.*

Studies have shown that, on the whole, sustainability does not unequivocally generate excess financial returns across the board.[30]

However, many specific sustainability indicators do correlate positively with certain financial performance metrics under certain timeframes, especially internal indicators tied to operational efficiency and resource management.[31] For example, companies that prioritize waste reduction and recycling often see lower operational costs and improved profit margins, translating to direct internal benefits. Similarly, strong labor practices can lead to higher employee satisfaction, which, in turn, may boost productivity and reduce turnover, subtly supporting financial performance. However, when viewed in aggregate, sustainability does not show a consistently strong correlation with financial outperformance, especially when causal links are examined. Existing research generally suggests a neutral relationship between sustainability and overall financial performance, particularly over the shorter-term investment horizons that many investors prioritize.

The complexity of the relationship also stems from the indirect nature of many sustainability benefits. Some sustainability practices may support a company's long-term resilience, reputation, and stakeholder trust—qualities that contribute to sustainable growth but may not yield immediate financial gains. For example, factors such as an enhanced reputation for environmental stewardship or high employee morale can influence brand equity, customer loyalty, employee turnover, and even risk management, potentially leading to long-term value creation.[32] Over time, as regulatory pressures around climate and environmental sustainability intensify, these indirect relationships could become more pronounced and measurable.

The weakest sustainability and corporate financial relationship is for companies deemed sustainable by virtue of inclusion in a sustainability-related mutual fund. In the United States, for instance, sustainability-focused funds often resemble traditional index funds in terms of performance. Despite this similarity, these sustainability (including ESG) funds typically charge higher fees, driven by their positioning as "sustainable" or "responsible" investment options. The rationale behind the higher fees is partly due to the additional resources required for sustainability research, assessment, and reporting. However, for investors seeking a return on investment that directly corresponds to higher fees, the benefits of sustainability funds may not be immediately clear.

In China, ESG funds are experiencing rapid growth, and in favorable market conditions, they appear to generate excess returns. This promising outlook has attracted the attention of investors seeking sustainable investments. However, a deeper analysis reveals that many of these funds exhibit a selection strategy closely aligned with growth-oriented funds rather than distinctly ESG-focused criteria. This overlap raises questions about the additional value that ESG funds offer in comparison to conventional growth investments. For example, one prominent ESG fund that delivered strong returns in 2020 allocated six out of its top ten holdings to liquor companies. This allocation diverges significantly from Western ESG standards, which often exclude industries such as alcohol, arms manufacturing, and gambling due to perceived social and environmental impacts. In contrast, Chinese ESG frameworks tend to adopt a more flexible approach, driven by domestic economic priorities and cultural factors. Liquor companies, for instance, may be seen as supporting local agriculture and employment, which can enhance their ESG appeal in the Chinese context.

This discrepancy between Western and Chinese ESG fund strategies highlights the challenge of developing globally standardized sustainability criteria. Although cultural differences undoubtedly shape sustainability perceptions and measures, the inclusion of industries such as liquor manufacturing in ESG portfolios can still prompt questions. It remains unclear why liquor companies, from a sustainability perspective, should receive a significantly higher rating than other sectors with potentially lower environmental and social risks.

While the current US administration retreats on ESG, American and global corporations continue to incorporate sustainability management. In America, some state and local governments continue to promote the green economy. Moreover, China's ESG landscape is moving forward. Many frameworks and guidelines such as the ones developed by the China Securities Regulatory Commission (CSRC) and the China Green Finance Committee provide a basis for ESG reporting and assessment in China. These standards often seek to align with national goals, such as economic growth, job creation, and social stability, potentially at the expense of stricter exclusions seen in some Western standards. Although the growth of ESG funds in China reflects increasing interest in sustainability, it also underscores the importance of adapting sustainability criteria to local conditions. For investors, understanding these nuances is crucial in assessing the sustainability credentials of the myriad of sustainability-focused funds globally.

Major Challenges

Despite the potential benefits of incorporating sustainability factors into financial decision-making, there are challenges in measuring and interpreting sustainability metrics. There is no universally accepted standard for ESG or sustainability ratings as we have outlined earlier, and different methodologies used by different rating agencies can lead to discrepancies in how sustainability performance is assessed. Additionally, some aspects of sustainability—such as social impacts or governance standards—are always difficult to quantify and standardize, and as we have illustrated in the case of China, these standards are often region and culture specific, making cross-comparisons very difficult. To address this issue, there is a growing call for more standardized and comprehensive sustainability measurement frameworks.

In addition, the growth of sustainability metrics also raises concerns about "greenwashing"—the practice of presenting a misleading impression of environmental responsibility without making meaningful changes. With increased scrutiny from investors, consumers, and regulatory bodies, companies overstating their sustainability efforts face growing reputational and legal risks. Therefore, failing to follow through on sustainability commitments can lead to distrust, reputational damage, and potentially even legal consequences if deceptive practices are exposed. We will discuss this issue in detail in chapter 6.

Another key challenge is the limited availability of long-term data on sustainability performance. Because ESG investing has gained traction only recently, there is still insufficient longitudinal data to conclusively determine whether sustainability practices consistently deliver stable and excess returns over time. Both ESG and sustainability are long-term concepts that extend beyond immediate financial performance, even encompassing ideas like intergenerational equity. Much of the existing research examines ESG within short-term frameworks, which may miss the broader and enduring benefits that sustainability initiatives can provide.

Environmental sustainability, for example, is inherently tied to longer time horizons, making short-term assessments insufficient to capture its full impact. Furthermore, financial markets require time to accurately measure and reflect the effects of sustainability practices on a company's overall valuation. Currently, stock market valuations largely overlook sustainability factors, as financial markets are primarily focused on risk and return. The industry is still in the early stages of developing methodologies for assessing climate risk and incorporating it into valuation models. Often, companies experience a period of financial realization before the market fully acknowledges the impact of sustainability factors on their value. As more data becomes available and valuation models evolve to better account for sustainability risks and rewards, we may gain clearer insights into sustainability's potential for long-term value creation.

Ultimately, understanding the true impact of sustainability on financial performance requires nuanced analysis, sector-specific considerations, and a clear framework for measuring the value of sustainability beyond immediate returns. As sustainability reporting standards continue to evolve and companies increasingly integrate sustainability into their core strategies, the ability to understand and capitalize on the connection between sustainability practices and financial success is likely to improve.

CONCLUSION

Sustainability management has been overblown by ideologues of the left and right. As with any management practice, there are few absolutes, and sustainability principles must be crafted to deal with specific situations. Scoring companies entirely on sustainability practices is a little ridiculous, but ignoring or opposing sustainability management is even worse. The practice of management has advanced dramatically over the past century. As we continue to note in this work, accounting, financial control systems, management information systems, just-in-time inventory control, international commerce, operations management, team management, and a host of other innovations have enabled managers to enhance productivity while dealing with an increasingly complex business environment. Sustainability management is simply another tool for managers seeking to deal with our rapidly changing world.

The argument against sustainability management is that these factors have nothing to do with generating revenues or reducing expenditures and that they distract companies from increasing profits and are therefore breaking the contract between shareholders and management. We have analyzed this argument in depth in this chapter. To some conservative politicos, sustainability considerations are extraneous and left-wing ideological principles. However, regardless of the politics, sustainability management is about effective management in the twenty-first century brain-based economy on a planet with over eight billion people. As Paul Simon once wrote, "One man's ceiling is another man's floor." New Yorkers, like Paul and the authors of this book, live in apartments and understand crowding. And this planet has gotten crowded. The need for precision and care in management is growing because the impact of mistakes is growing. There was a time when you could dump garbage in the ocean, knowing it would decompose and biodegrade. After the invention of plastics and chemicals that were durable and long-lasting for commercial use, waste no longer degraded in the environment, and its disposal and treatment became more complex and costly. We benefit enormously from new chemical technologies, but their use often creates environmental issues that must be addressed. If we are going to continue to advance our economy through the development of new technologies, we must learn how to manage those technologies so they do not cause harm to people and the planet.

In many cases, the argument seems to be less against sustainability management than about using ESG factors to guide investment. Investments should never rely on single indicators, as we outlined at the beginning of this chapter. The measurement of organizational use of environment, social impact, and corporate governance practices is still in its infancy. We are at about the same place that financial accounting was in the mid-1930s. On the environmental side of the equation, we have not yet developed generally accepted environmental sustainability metrics. The same is true of measures capturing the use of corporate governance, inclusiveness, and community impact principles.

But delegitimizing ESG factors is at least as bad as misusing and misunderstanding their measurement. We need to get better at understanding these issues and managing organizations in ways that reduce environmental damage, enhance host community impact, and increase organizational brainpower. Most senior managers with business and law backgrounds do not understand environmental issues. The graduate programs we teach at Columbia University in sustainability management (established in 2010) and environmental science and policy (established in 2002) have now educated over three thousand sustainability professionals who do understand sustainability issues. Programs at Arizona State, Yale, Bard, the New School, NYU, Harvard, American University, UC Santa Barbara's Bren School of Management, Duke, LSE, Stanford, and the University of Toronto (among others) have educated thousands more. These new sustainability professionals have the training needed to turn ESG from aspirational goals to organizational deeds.

We are at the start of a new era of management. But we have a lot to learn. Some progressives place too much faith in our ability to manage sustainability, and some conservatives fail to grasp the importance of these issues to the corporate bottom line. It is sad or perhaps comical when state legislators who know little about management and even less about science try to legislate against what they have decided is "woke" management or "woke" investment. But it is also dangerous to overestimate our ability to manage according to sustainability principles. We are learning, and we are getting better. But we have a long way to go, and a little humility is definitely called for. We are optimistic about our progress but caution against overconfidence. The attack on ESG must be repelled, and the best defense is results and improved organizational performance.

4

INTEGRATING SUSTAINABILITY MANAGEMENT INTO ORGANIZATIONAL MANAGEMENT

This chapter explores the process of integrating sustainability management into the core of organizational management, which is expected to drive a transformative approach to organizational operations. Sustainability management requires more self-conscious and mindful community engagements, more transparent organizational governance, and more thoughtful production and consumption processes designed to reduce negative environmental impacts. We discuss how this integration enhances organizational performance and profits and enables organizations to meet the growing expectations of stakeholders for responsible environmental and community stewardship. Sustainability practices change across organizational functions, so it is important to understand how the application of sustainability performance indicators varies according to organizational goals. This chapter offers an evaluation of common challenges faced by organizations when integrating sustainability into routine organizational management, how to overcome them, and how to leverage sustainability as a competitive advantage. It provides an overview of case studies on organizations that have succeeded in integrating and "normalizing" sustainability management.

HOW CAN SUSTAINABILITY BE MADE AN ORGANIZATIONAL ROUTINE?

A necessary but not sufficient step to make sustainability an organizational routine is the development of sustainability metrics and their integration into the organization's overall performance measurement system and key performance indicators. This has been detailed in the preceding chapter. Without specific sustainability measures, it is not clear how sustainability is operationally defined. Once the operational definition is in place, sustainability becomes a form of management innovation. The issue is: What needs to happen in the organization to bring about this particular management innovation? The first issue is to determine where or in what part of the organization the function should be initiated and initially overseen. When sustainability is brought into the organization, it should be seen as an innovative set of new tasks that must be developed and then learned. Training, resource allocation, and reinforcement are needed to ensure that this new function is absorbed into the organization.[1]

The organizational home for these activities may be a distinct sustainability unit that has sufficient resources and authority to analyze operations throughout the organization and develop work processes and facilities to reduce environmental impacts, save energy, recruit brainpower, and analyze and reduce negative community impacts. Alternatively, it could be a temporary working group convened directly by the CEO or COO and reporting directly to the top manager until the innovation is institutionalized.

At the beginning stages, an organization must analyze its operations and develop a strategy for increasing environmental and other types of sustainability. This analytic and strategic function must then be backed up with the resources and authority to bring about innovative practices. To be effective, organizational members need to be convinced that the operation benefits from the innovation.

That change process is complex and often an object of resistance, with the typical argument being, "If it's not broken, why fix it?"

It is particularly important that the CEO, COO, and other key organizational leaders support sustainability.[2] That support must be present in normal organizational communications—both internal and external. It should be visible in the organization's web and social media presence. Most critically, there needs to be evidence of resource allocation for this new function. Access to key decision-makers is also important early on. Because resistance to change is normal, the perception that top management is committed (or indifferent) can make or break organizational innovations like sustainability.

THE ARGUMENT FOR SUSTAINABILITY AS A MANAGEMENT PRINCIPLE

If we think of sustainability or environmental, social, and governance (ESG) standards as a management concept rather than as an element of ideology, we have a better chance of establishing its practice in an organization. Starting with environmental impact and risk, a company that does not understand and measure its impact on ecosystems, as well as the risk to its operations posed by climate change and climate-accelerated extreme weather events, is a poorly managed operation. Fossil fuel companies and shipping companies have extreme exposure to environmental and climate risks.[3] If you doubt our assessment of fossil fuel ecological risk, consider BP's expenses resulting from their 2010 Gulf of Mexico disaster.[4] If you question the need to understand transport risk, ask Norfolk Southern how much they think the derailment in East Palestine, Ohio, is going to cost them and their shareholders.[5] Moreover, we live on a more crowded and interdependent planet, and every organization must be cognizant of the potential liability they could incur if they poison their neighbors or customers. An organization that understands its exposure to environmental risk is likely to be better at understanding and managing its exposure to other risks. By cutting railroad staff and fighting safety rules, Norfolk Southern seemed to be inviting risk: Shouldn't an investor be aware of these practices? Better awareness of risk should lead to lower levels of risk and less exposure to catastrophic financial loss. Mindfulness of environmental risk is as important as the attention paid to financial fraud or corruption. The focus is on the potential downside risk of an organization's operations.

Similarly, consider a corporation's governance structure and its hiring practices. An organization that privileges one race, gender, religion, sexual orientation, or national origin over another reduces the pool of talent it can draw on to staff and manage the operation. We are in a brain-based economy. The high value-added parts of the economy and the greatest profits are in the organizations or parts of organizations that are creative, analytic, and innovative. There's more money in software than hardware. As manufactured products become commodities, they are subject to competitive forces that tend to limit profits. That is why IBM stopped making personal computers and sold the ThinkPad brand to Lenovo.[6] A diverse board and diverse workers will provide the benefit of more brainpower and different life experiences to address organizational challenges. A less diverse organization tends to stimulate insularity and groupthink. Being aware of the value of diversity is an indicator of management excellence. In a global competition for innovation, customers, and profits, a diverse team that is built on the best talent is likely to beat the team that is more homogeneous but less talented. Note that the definition of diversity we are using is not race, gender, or ethnicity based but focused on diverse life experiences.

Well-managed organizations in the twenty-first century require sustainability management. In America, over 80 percent of our gross domestic product (GDP) is in the service economy,[7] and when we manufacture food, clothing, shelter, and any other goods in America, much of that manufacturing requires automation and other forms of advanced technology. Modern farming utilizes satellite data, automation, and artificial intelligence to optimize the use of water, fertilizer, and pesticides. Advanced engineering, logistics, targeted marketing, and new communication channels require constant organizational learning and the continuous development and modification of organizational routines and practices. As we continue to note, we live in a brain-based economy. Organizations must compete for the best brains if they are to succeed in the competitive marketplace.

If the organization's culture is gender biased, racist, xenophobic, homophobic, or biased in any way other than fit for the job, it is artificially limiting the universe of talent it can recruit. In our view, that is a form of inadequate management. If an organization's governing council meets in secret and does not disclose who makes decisions and why they've been made, then its governance risks decisions that are myopic and poorly vetted, and that, too, is an indication of inadequate management.

Finally, there is the issue of an organization's ability to understand and address its impact on the community it operates in. As we note several times in this book, Amazon tried to locate its HQ2 in Long Island City, New York, but misunderstood the political climate, got greedy, and negotiated a $3 billion siting subsidy from New York State and City.[8] The community and local politicos were enraged, and eventually the political opposition in New York compelled Amazon to site their operation in suburban Washington, DC. Of course, since then, they've halted construction of HQ2 and quietly added thousands of staff to sites scattered around New York City. Nevertheless, the political disaster in Long Island City damaged the company's image and was not an indicator of sophisticated management. Shaking down a city with sixty thousand homeless people seemed a little ridiculous from a company as rich and successful as Amazon. Eventually, and to many positive reviews, Amazon converted the old Lord and Taylor retail building on Fifth Avenue to a workspace for two thousand creative and management staff and has quietly built up its New York presence over the past several years. It appears they have learned some lessons about the complexity of New York's political environment and how to operate effectively in that environment. Amazon wants to be in New York City because of the talented labor the city attracts. Community impact is a critical element of organizational sustainability.

Each community an organization operates in is different, and some organizations are better at navigating difficult environments. For example, there are nineteen Targets in New York City, four Costcos, but no Walmarts. Walmart is the largest American retailer. It has a terrific record on environmental sustainability. Although it has over 4,700 stores, they have not penetrated New York City's political environment. Costco and Target seem to have figured it out a while ago, whereas Walmart remains on the outside.

We saw another horrific example of terrible corporate-community relations after the catastrophic train accident in Ohio in 2023. Norfolk Southern and the US government were slow in responding to the toxic accident.[9] They misplayed their engagement with the community and compounded the physical and environmental disaster with a complete failure of community relations. Residents were traumatized and correctly believed they were mistreated by a large and successful corporation. Coupled with government's regulatory and response failure, the combination of private and public incompetence exacerbated the damage suffered by the community.

Modern organizations with instant communication and high-speed transmission of information are correctly expected to move quickly to respond to disaster. The absence of capacity to interact with the local community is another indicator of terrible management. Yes, the railroad is making money. But for how long, with such poor safety practices and inadequate capacity to manage community relations? The company seemed to be improvising their response in Ohio instead of implementing a carefully planned post-disaster cleanup and community relations program. The East Palestine case does not make one want to run out and buy shares in Norfolk Southern.

If the organization does not consider its impact on the local community, then it may find its ability to expand compromised—this lack of political sensitivity is also an indication of inadequate management. And finally, if an organization does not understand and seek to reduce its impact on the planet, it may find itself regulated and policed into crisis, bankruptcy, or nonexistence.

CLIMATE REPORTING, SUSTAINABILITY METRICS, AND SUSTAINABILITY MANAGEMENT

One of the critical developments expediting the integration of sustainability metrics with sustainability management is the requirement that private corporations report their carbon emissions and climate risks. Although, as of this writing, formal reporting requirements required by the US Securities and Exchange Commission (SEC) were first challenged in court in the United States[10] and then discarded by the second Trump administration, they are still being implemented in the European Union and the state of California. Despite the delay experienced during the second Trump administration, we believe that these requirements will ultimately be established in the United States.

About two years after releasing its draft regulation in 2022, the SEC issued its final climate disclosure rule.[11] Although the new rule was controversial, challenged in the courts, and halted by the second Trump administration, it remains an important step in the development of the field of sustainability management.

In 2024, the SEC faced a political deadline to issue their climate disclosure regulation due to the uncertainty caused by the 2024 presidential and congressional elections. They really had no choice and finally acted on March 6, 2024. Later that month, they froze enforcement during court challenges. According to the SEC's website in 2024:

> The Securities and Exchange Commission today [March 6, 2024] adopted rules to enhance and standardize climate-related disclosures by public companies and in public offerings. The final rules reflect the Commission's efforts to respond to investors' demand for more consistent, comparable, and reliable information about the financial effects of climate-related risks on a registrant's operations and how it manages those risks while balancing concerns about mitigating the associated costs of the rules. "Our federal securities laws lay out a basic bargain. Investors get to decide which risks they want

> to take so long as companies raising money from the public make what President Franklin Roosevelt called 'complete and truthful disclosure,'" said SEC Chair Gary Gensler. "Over the last 90 years, the SEC has updated, from time to time, the disclosure requirements underlying that basic bargain and, when necessary, provided guidance with respect to those disclosure requirements." Chair Gensler added, "These final rules build on past requirements by mandating material climate risk disclosures by public companies and in public offerings. The rules will provide investors with consistent, comparable, and decision-useful information, and issuers with clear reporting requirements. Further, they will provide specificity on what companies must disclose, which will produce more useful information than what investors see today. They will also require that climate risk disclosures be included in a company's SEC filings, such as annual reports and registration statements rather than on company websites, which will help make them more reliable."[12]

The final rules reflected over 24,000 comments and intense debate about what was reasonable and necessary. Environmentalists were unhappy about the omission of reporting on Scope 3 emissions (emissions from an organization's supply chain). Conservatives believed the entire effort to report on environmental risk was outside the mandate of the SEC. We view Trump's abandonment of carbon reporting as a temporary setback.

Rulemaking, like budgeting, has a strategic logic. When an agency proposes a budget, they know that their request will be cut and certainly they'll never get more than they ask for. So, their initial request leaves room for cuts that can be easily absorbed. Similarly, *in the regulatory process, proposed regulations are nearly always more stringent than the final regulations*. Regulators know to put everything on the table so they can give up some provisions and still retain a workable rule. Later, once the new rule is in effect, revisions based on operational experience or possibly new scientific findings tend to make the rule more stringent. The goal with a new regulation is to get your foot in the door, establish the legitimacy of the rule, and then work over time to improve it.

In our view, even though now abandoned, the SEC rule was a first step in codifying the measurement of the environmental impact of publicly traded corporations. On a more crowded and environmentally stressed planet, investors need to know the environmental risks posed by their investments. Climate is only one of these environmental risks. Reduced biodiversity, infectious diseases, toxics, and other forms of environmental damage caused by corporations or potentially caused by others but impacting corporate functioning also pose *financial* risks to investors. The SEC's actions during the Biden administration were a watershed moment in legitimizing sustainability metrics, a key step in helping us learn how to manage our economic growth without destroying our planet. Its delay by the second Trump administration is a bump in the road, and the vacuum it created is being filled by state-level reporting requirements on American companies and the reporting requirements mandated by the European Union on the thousands of American companies doing business in Europe.

Before the European Union and California greenhouse gas disclosure rules were promulgated, every company raising capital in America's public marketplace could release whatever environmental information they wanted to release. This was the situation with financial data leading up to the stock market crash of 1929. Back then, companies reported whatever financial information they felt like releasing. The lack of reliable information turned the stock market into a casino. This ended with the New Deal's creation of the SEC in the 1930s. The SEC defined financial reporting, which led to the development of the profession of financial accounting and the job of chief financial officer (CFO). SEC rules on corporate reporting have been evolving since the 1930s. Our view is that even the now-abandoned actions taken by the SEC in 2024 accelerated the rise of the field of environmental accounting and facilitated the development of standardized sustainability metrics. The rulemaking process identified practical issues with the proposed rule and resulted in a more modest but defensible final rule. Our view is that, eventually, that rule, or one like it, will be implemented by the US government.

Measurement of greenhouse gas emissions is complicated—certainly more complex than measuring revenues and expenditures. Corporate reporting to the SEC has evolved to include disclosure of potential conflicts of interest of corporate boards, as well as other rules to reduce the possibility of self-dealing and fraud. Assuming the carbon rule is revived after Trump and survives the conservative court system and the appeals it will then confront, the regulation will accelerate our ability to refine these measures and base management decision-making on steps that enable the most cost-effective pollution reductions feasible. The elimination of Scope 3 emissions from the rule was in part a response to the difficulty of one organization measuring greenhouse gases emitted by another organization that they do not control.[13] But if every organization in the supply chain is eventually required to report their own Scope 1 and 2 emissions, eventually emissions in a supply chain would be more accurately estimated. Because the supply chain is global and the SEC rule was limited to the United States, the accurate measurement of Scope 3 emissions may well be a long time in coming. But what is important is that government's regulation of corporate environmental reporting has finally begun.

Our only objection to the now-abandoned SEC disclosure rule was that it was limited to climate risk and did not encompass the full range of environmental risk. Of course, the second Trump SEC objected to the very idea of corporate sustainability reporting. The need for a broader framework of environmental sustainability metrics was highlighted in a March 2022 *Wall Street Journal* interview conducted by reporter Ed Ballard of Alison Bewick, the head of risk management at Nestle. According to Ballard:

> A Nestlé SA executive who helped put together a new framework for biodiversity reporting said that companies should release integrated disclosures related to climate change and nature, because the two things are so interconnected. Alison Bewick, head of risk management at Nestlé, was one of the executives involved in creating the initial framework from the Taskforce on Nature-related Financial Disclosures. . . . The framework, devised by businesses working in

> collaboration with scientific organizations and nonprofit sustainability standard-setters, is meant to serve as a guide for companies about reporting on nature-related risks and opportunities. It follows the model of the climate-risk framework devised by the Task Force on Climate-Related Financial Disclosures.[14]

As Bewick clearly understands, the overall issue is environmental risk. Climate change is seen by some as the most important risk and an "existential" threat as well, but it's a little silly to hold a contest between environmental risks. At any one time, any number of risks could threaten us. Due to the war in Ukraine, we started to think about the risk of radioactive contamination from nuclear power plants damaged by war.[15] We are still living through the risk posed by an invasive virus called COVID-19. There are no shortages of environmental risks caused by the unanticipated impacts of modern technology. Nestle's Bewick concretely calls for integrating the biodiversity measurement and disclosure framework with the climate framework. In the *Wall Street Journal* interview, she observed that, "When we think about how we can address our carbon footprint, a lot of it's through nature-based solutions. It's beyond just the greenhouse-gas measurement, it's around the availability of water, it could be the soil profile, how you approach land-use in terms of rotation of crops, that type of thing. I think the underlying principle is that this should be ultimately an integrated disclosure, because there's a very strong interconnectivity and dependency between nature and climate."[16]

The resistance to climate science we see in the political world and in fossil fuel companies reminds us of the resistance to medical science's connection between smoking tobacco and cancer. The relationship is clear and has been established for many years, but economic interests continue to dominate health concerns. In 2019, 1.1 billion people smoked, and 7.7 million people died from tobacco-related illness.[17] Climate change is similar, and if anything, the economic interests threatened are far more powerful than the tobacco industry. Perhaps that is why climate change is such a dominant environmental issue. Mitigating climate change requires fundamental changes in the technologies that drive our economic system.

Climate science is relatively straightforward, and some of the impacts of climate change are well understood. But at a certain point, the relatively simple physics of climate change intersects with far more complex biological and ecological systems. Those changes and the damage to ecosystems caused by non-climate-related human impacts are not as well understood and are far more difficult to measure. The web of relationships in the living world of ecology is more subtle and complex than the massive impact of greenhouse gases on our climate. And yet millions of subtle changes to our biosphere can add up to an impact easily as massive as that caused by climate change.

Bewick's call for integrating climate and biodiversity measures in a single framework makes sense because the two sets of impacts are interconnected. It is also a way for the relatively less "popular" biodiversity impacts to cash in on the currency and "fame" of climate impacts. What is most important is that we get beyond this improvisational stage in environmental sustainability metrics. In the world of corporate finance, accounting terms are defined and regulated by the government, not by nongovernmental organizations (NGOs). When the SEC was created during the New Deal, its evolving role led to the development of generally accepted accounting practices. The SEC, under Biden, started the process of developing generally accepted environmental sustainability metrics with their carbon disclosure rule. If these are to become routine elements of corporate disclosure, companies need clear definitions of what they must disclose. What begins with climate disclosures should eventually expand into broader measures of environmental impact and risk.

The aim of the stalled SEC rule was precisely to provide clearer metrics for climate disclosure. According to Richard Vanderford's report in the *Wall Street Journal*, "The [SEC Climate Disclosure] rule is meant to bring order to what has been uneven climate reporting by different public companies. In place of voluntary sustainability reports which use handpicked metrics, companies would have to disclose in much greater detail how much carbon they emit and how they plan to address looming climate risks. In theory, investors could then make more informed comparisons of businesses."[18]

There is little question that adding sustainability metrics to management will be complicated, and we will make mistakes as we learn how to do this. Just as financial reporting keeps accounting firms in business, complying with environmental sustainability metric reporting requirements will cost companies serious amounts of cash and fund a growing profession of sustainability professionals. But if we want to grow our economy without destroying our planet, we need to do a better job of measuring and managing our environmental impacts.

Our view is that all competent managers must be sustainability managers, and therefore, the profession of sustainability management should eventually be subsumed by the profession of management. Of course, it could happen the other way around, and the only type of management taught in business and public policy schools will be sustainability management. No manager would be considered competent if they could not read or understand a balance sheet or a financial control system. A manager who ignores the cost of energy or waste and ignores potential environmental liability should also be considered incompetent.

Accounting was developed as a critical management profession in the mid-twentieth century, resulting in the creation of the position of CFO in many organizations. At the end of the century, we saw a similar development as information management became central, leading to the rise of chief information officers (CIOs) in many large organizations. In this century, we are starting to see the development of organizational units that work to promote the principles of environmental sustainability. Today, most of those running sustainability units are trained in other fields. As they retire, they will be replaced by well-trained sustainability professionals.

THE PROCESS OF INTEGRATING SUSTAINABILITY INTO MANAGEMENT

Financial issues, performance issues, marketing issues, technological issues, and organizational capacity are all critical elements that factor into management decision-making. These factors are seamlessly integrated into decision-making because they have been proven over time to be connected to organizational success. Sustainability issues are at the start of this integration process, and the degree of incorporation varies. Some managers see environmental sustainability as central to organizational success, and others consider the full range of ESG issues as central. Other managers consider them peripheral. To some degree, this is an empirical issue that will be proven or disproven over time.

Just as these traditional issues are addressed through routine management functions, the goal is for sustainability to take its place as simply another routine performed in most organizations. The process of absorbing these new routines and their relative priority will be situationally determined. Different types of organizations in different physical, political, economic, and cultural locations will approach sustainability differently. Because management is a craft, these functions need to be tailored to each situation with the overarching goal of creating an organization more mindful of its surroundings and its impact on those surroundings.

Many organizations have begun the process of integrating sustainability into management. According to Lindsay Beltzer of the Conference Board:

> Companies are addressing multiple priorities in the area of sustainability: identifying issues that are key to their particular company; integrating sustainability into their business strategy and operations; setting and rewarding against environmental, social and governance (ESG) goals; organizing to achieve these aims at the board and management levels; and communicating their sustainability story more effectively—all while dealing with increased regulation, demanding

> ESG rating agencies, and evolving reporting frameworks. The key to long-term success, however, lies in embedding sustainability into their cultural DNA so that everyone, from the C-Suite to frontline workers, thinks and acts with sustainability in mind. A sustainability culture has the potential not only to help reduce costs by saving money in areas such as energy, water, and waste, but also in identifying and pursuing innovations and new business opportunities. At the heart of this effort is upskilling—equipping employees with new or advanced skills to improve their job performance—a trend that is becoming more common, with 69 percent of companies doing more skill building now than before the COVID-19 pandemic. Similarly to digital upskilling, upskilling in sustainability will require bringing specialized knowledge and skills such as carbon accounting, carbon removal and ecosystem services valuation into the workplace. It will also necessitate new ways of looking at the company's business, while integrating sustainability into the company's existing culture.[19]

The Conference Board has reported that a large number of American corporations have begun this work, and it is advancing rapidly in Europe as well. In Columbia's graduate course in sustainability management, we have now collected over six hundred case studies of organizations seeking to integrate sustainability into their operations. These case studies are the final paper in a graduate course. These cases, coupled with those published by the Conference Board, provide additional evidence of the trend to add sustainability and ESG to organizational management systems.

The world and the global economy are increasingly complex and interdependent. Navigating that complexity requires creative and innovative strategic thinking and care in understanding the causes and effects of organizational behavior. Organizations that have incorporated sustainability into their management routines tend to be careful and conscious of their actions. Sustainability is a means toward the goals of organizations, not self-justifying principles of an ideology of "correct behavior." Environmental sustainability should now be seen as a subfield of sustainability management, which today includes issues such as management and staff diversity, transparent organizational governance, and the organization's impact on its surrounding community or communities.

The notion of diversity and inclusion as an ideology rather than as a management principle relates to how diversity is defined and conceptualized. For people motivated by ideology, diversity is the goal itself and is self-justifying. Diversity is pursued because it is right and ethical. We have sympathy for this view because we consider exclusion based on race, religion, ethnicity, or national origin to be unethical. However, in management terms, diversity is *utilized* to ensure the organization's staff and management bring a wide variety of perspectives to the organization's work. Merit is still sought in recruiting the team, but the *definition* of merit is broadened to ensure the people hired have different lived experiences. Diversity is a means and not an end.

Similarly, a concern for environmental impact is also utilized as a cost-cutting measure to save the costs of resources like energy and water and to reduce the risks of environmental liability. But perhaps the most telling indication of the growth of sustainability as a fundamental management principle is a 2024 study of corporate management effectiveness conducted by the Drucker Institute of the Claremont Graduate School. The highlights of the study appeared in a recent piece by Rick Wartzman and Kelly Tang of Bendable Labs in the *Wall Street Journal*. According to Wartzman and Tang:[20]

> All sorts of companies from different industries have been staffing up to help their customers meet carbon-emissions and waste-reduction targets and comply with a welter of environmental regulations, as well as ensure that they meet their own climate goals and that their supply chains aren't disrupted by extreme-weather events and energy shortages. What's notable is that, according to our research, these businesses are generally better managed than those that aren't dedicating the same level of resources to such matters. Our findings are derived from a measure of corporate effectiveness created by the Drucker Institute at Claremont Graduate University. The institute's statistical model, which rests on the core principles of the late professor and author Peter Drucker, forms the basis of

> the Management Top 250, an annual ranking produced in partnership with *The Wall Street Journal*. . . . In our most recent analysis, we wanted to determine whether there was a connection between the number of climate-related jobs that a company has, relative to the size of its overall workforce, and how well-managed it is by our reckoning. . . . In all, we use 34 metrics to evaluate how companies perform, using standardized scores with a typical range of 0 to 100 and a mean of 50, across five areas: customer satisfaction, innovation, social responsibility, employee engagement and development, and financial strength. These categories then roll up into a score that indicates a company's total effectiveness. Drucker defined effectiveness as "doing the right things well."

In this view, sustainability is an element of management effectiveness. There is an undeniable ideological current in some versions of sustainability management, and that is what has generated the reaction against what right-wing ideologues term "woke management." This is related to climate extremists who spray paint artwork, chain themselves to coal-fired power plants, and work to shame people who fly in private planes or work for fossil fuel companies. In this sense, environmental concern is utilized to attack people seen as an enemy and as a form of power politics rather than as an effort to genuinely seek a method to reduce the environmental impact of economic production. When sustainability is seen as an element of effective management, it is simply a form of careful production that seeks to ensure that the negative impacts of production are minimized and positive impacts maximized.

Of course, to do this, management must develop and utilize scientific expertise on environmental damage. The science of toxicology, ecology, air and water pollution, or climate can't be ignored or wished away. It must be included in management decision-making just as data on market share, revenues, expenses, and earnings before interest, taxes, and amortization (EBITA) is utilized by management. Environmental impact needs to be understood because just as the number of sustainability employees relates to organizational effectiveness, an understanding of an organization's environmental impact is a crucial piece of information that enables an organization to understand its vulnerability to environmental risk.

Management requires more sophistication because the world has become more crowded and complicated. We are deluged by information because the cost of computing and communication continues to be reduced, and our need for information seems limitless. Managers need information to measure the conditions they must navigate. In fact, as complexity grows, we are even looking for means of augmenting human intelligence with artificial intelligence. This is a sharp contrast from the middle of the twentieth century when we counted inventory by hand, recorded it on column pads, and calculated it on adding machines with rolls of paper that printed our results. Today, we use bar codes, smartphones, computers, and algorithms to count what we've sold and *project* what we should order. Management must be constantly aware of changing markets and conditions, and organizational behavior is expected to be capable of rapid change.

ESG ideology and other forms of principled advocacy play an important role in the world but should never be confused with pragmatic, goal-seeking sustainability management. Companies may reduce the visibility of ESG and DEI initiatives due to political blowback, but the essential importance of sustainability to effective management needs to be understood. Sustainability management is a requirement of effective management. Its opposite is sloppy, careless, shortsighted, and ineffective management. Political leaders and pundits can pretend that the world is not getting warmer, but business leaders do not have the luxury of indulging in ideologically induced fantasy.

EXAMPLES OF ORGANIZATIONS INTEGRATING SUSTAINABILITY INTO OPERATIONS AND THEIR BUSINESS PLANS

This chapter concludes with brief case studies of three corporations that have integrated sustainability into elements of their operations and product lines. The companies discussed are Apple, Chloé, and BlackRock.

Apple

Apple Inc. has integrated sustainability into its core operations, reducing toxic chemicals, limiting greenhouse gas emissions, and pursuing environmental justice throughout its global supply chain. It is serious about sustainability due to its customer base and its leadership team. The company has made substantial progress, achieving carbon neutrality for its global operations in 2020 and setting a target to be entirely carbon neutral across its entire value chain by 2030. It transitioned to 100 percent renewable energy in its corporate facilities, retail stores, and data centers and is increasingly using recycled materials, working to ensure that all products will eventually be made with 100 percent recycled or renewable materials. It has also incentivized rigorous supplier responsibility standards, with over 320 suppliers now committed to using 100 percent renewable energy.

Under the leadership of Tim Cook and Lisa Jackson, Apple has solidified its position as a leader in corporate sustainability. Cook and Jackson have overseen green bond issuances of $4.7 billion, directing proceeds toward environmental and climate initiatives. Jackson has led initiatives that have resulted in an over 60 percent reduction in carbon emissions across Apple's value chain since 2015. This is notable progress against the company's goal to reduce emissions across Apple's value chain by 75 percent in the same time period, as part of their 2030 carbon neutrality commitment.

Their leadership has ensured that sustainability is not just an operational goal but a fundamental aspect of Apple's business strategy. Jackson's history and role indicate Apple's deep commitment to environmental sustainability. After decades of government service, Jackson served as New Jersey's commissioner of environmental protection and then served for four years as the administrator of the Environmental Protection Agency (EPA) under President Barack Obama. She is now part of the executive management team of Apple and is considered a powerful insider and key advisor to CEO Tim Cook.

On the nonenvironmental aspects of sustainability, Cook and Jackson have achieved significant progress in diversity, equity, and inclusion by showing a 64 percent increase in the number of female and minority employees in leadership roles since 2014. The company has invested over $200 million in its Racial Equity and Justice Initiative, focusing on education, economic empowerment, and criminal justice reform. Apple's commitment to transparency is demonstrated through its comprehensive Environmental Responsibility Reports, which align with global frameworks such as the Global Reporting Initiative (GRI), the Sustainability Accounting Standards Board (SASB), and the Task Force on Climate-Related Financial Disclosures (TCFD), providing stakeholders with clear insights into its ESG performance. They have supported government efforts to establish mandatory greenhouse gas disclosures.

Apple devotes substantial resources to measuring their organization's sustainability and has clearly integrated sustainability into routine management decision-making. Writing in Apple's 2025 Environmental Progress Report, Jackson provided the following reflection:

> Every year, teams across our company find new and innovative ways to make our technology better for people and the planet. That progress has brought us closer than ever to Apple 2030: our goal to become carbon neutral for our global footprint, including our supply chain and the energy our customers use to power their devices.
>
> Thanks to these efforts, I'm proud to share that Apple has now cut our overall emissions by more than 60 percent since 2015. This report covers the work that makes a milestone like that possible. It describes in detail how we continue to dramatically reduce our climate impact, while helping accelerate a global transition toward recycled materials and renewable energy.
>
> Since 2018, we've powered every Apple facility with renewable energy—including our offices, retail stores, and data centers. That progress is quickly making its way across our global supply chain, and today, our suppliers now support more than 17.8 gigawatts of clean energy around the world.

> But our commitment doesn't end there. We're also investing in clean energy projects to match the energy our customers use to charge their devices. And with our Power for Impact program, we've launched renewable energy projects in countries including the Philippines, Thailand, and South Africa. By expanding access to safe, reliable electricity, we can protect the planet and support the communities most significantly impacted by climate change.
>
> To drive down carbon emissions even further, we're using more recycled materials than ever before. We now use 99 percent recycled rare earth elements in the magnets across our products. We've also continued to scale the use of recycled materials like tungsten, aluminum, cobalt, gold, and lithium. And we've done all that while making our products even more durable and easy to repair, because technology that lasts longer is better for the environment and our customers' wallets.[21]

Two features are notable from Jackson's reflections in Apple's 2024 report. First, she begins by referring to the hard work of teams throughout the company. This is a clear indication of the centrality of sustainability in Apple's corporate culture. The second is the presence of a series of sustainability metrics, including material recycled, greenhouse gas emissions, and the use of renewable energy.

Of course, there are critics of Apple's environmental record. In a 2023 piece in the *Washington Post*, Bloomberg's Mark Gongloff observed:

> Apple Inc.'s true specialty isn't consumer technology. It's marketing. Few other enterprises in human history have managed to efficiently separate people from their money at such scale. . . . But the credibility of Apple's environmental claims is a little fuzzier than the razzle-dazzle would have you believe. . . . Some of Apple's choices will also do clear and measurable good. Ditching leather, for example, is big: Cattle ranching is responsible for 14.5 percent of the planet's emissions, by one estimate. Committing to renewable energy and setting aggressive targets for emissions reduction are important. Grid Forecast could nudge electricity use in a positive direction. And the sheer

> volume of recycled materials in Apple's iPhones and other products is genuinely impressive. After that, the promises get murkier. . . . Apple's emissions goals depend heavily on carbon offsets, which are credits companies and people get for investing in projects to reduce carbon—often, planting trees. . . . More than 300 of Apple's suppliers have vowed to use 100 percent clean energy, but many can hit that goal only by using "renewable energy certificates," another type of credit.[22]

It is not realistic for everyone to move to 100 percent renewable energy when 60 percent of the world's electricity is generated by fossil fuels. But as the world transitions, the use of environmental attributes can be an important tool to bring investment into a market that needs to grow. These environmental attributes also create flexibility to source renewable and clean electricity beyond the relatively simple exercise of putting solar on a rooftop, which does not achieve the scale needed in the face of climate change. Therefore, it is reasonable for companies committed to sustainability to combine their own renewable energy generation with renewable energy certificates (RECs). Apple views the strategic use of well-designed REC origins as an important interim solution to longer-term procurement options like green tariffs or power purchase agreements, which are becoming increasingly available across the globe.

We note that Apple only applies clean electricity—not carbon offsets—against its electricity footprint. Apple has limited the use of carbon offsets to meet environmental goals to its residual footprint, which they have described at 25 percent of their 2015 baseline; this corresponds directly to their goal of reducing emissions by 75 percent. Apple has stated that these reduction pathways are aligned with a 1.5C global pathway. Additionally, Apple is vocal about the challenges within the voluntary market for carbon credits, including quality and scale. In 2021, the company created the Restore Fund with Goldman Sachs and Conservation International to help scale investment in high-quality nature-based carbon projects. The Restore Fund has since been expanded, and Apple has published details on the measures in place to ensure the quality and integrity of the carbon removal credits generated through the fund's investments.

It is true that Apple's hardware manufacturing involves massive amounts of material production and consumption, but even critics recognize the effort that Apple has devoted to sustainability. Within Gongloff's critique of Apple's environmental record, he also notes that "these days, corporate 'wokeism' attracts conservative backlash. . . . Apple deserves kudos for making as much noise about its social values as possible. In this, at least, the company is on the right side of history, setting a good example for its peers."[23]

On corporate culture, communications strategy, and sustainability metrics, Apple demonstrates a serious commitment to sustainability management. It is not perfect, but it is substantial and quite real in not only statements but also quantified progress against clear goals.

Chloé

The luxury fashion house Chloé has integrated sustainability into its operations in a robust and multifaceted way, reflecting a deep commitment to environmental and social responsibility. It has made significant strides, such as achieving B-Corp certification and transforming into a mission-driven company with clear social and environmental objectives. Chloé's vision includes four pillars: people, sourcing, planet, and communities. The company is trying to ensure that it addresses both environmental and nonenvironmental sustainability elements such as social justice, DEI, corporate reporting, and safety.

Chloé is working to embed sustainability into its core business strategy. Chloé's current efforts involve regular monitoring of key sustainability metrics, active participation in ESG initiatives, and routine communication of goals and progress. For example, their goal to reduce 25 percent of greenhouse gas emissions per product and offset 100 percent of emissions by 2025 is evidence of a quantifiable, metric-based commitment to climate action. Chloé is trying to enhance the opportunities of 150,000 girls through the GIRLS

FORWARD partnership with UNICEF by raising money to provide education, entrepreneurship, and training programs in Bolivia, Jordan, Morocco, Senegal, and Tajikistan. Additionally, Chloé is donating 1 percent of their annual revenue to support gender equality. Also, they have set three objectives to reach their sourcing goal: "reach more than 90 percent lower impact products, 30 percent of Fair Trade & social impact sourcing on all categories and transparency & traceability protocol on 100 percent of our products."[24]

The effectiveness of Chloé's sustainability integration depends on the consistent achievement of a set of ambitious goals. The introduction of tools like social profit and loss (SP&L) and regular social and environmental audits indicate that Chloé is serious about tracking and improving its sustainability performance across the value chain. Yet, whether these measures are "enough" remains to be seen and will require transparent reporting and accountability to ensure that the company meets its targets and truly drives positive change within the industry.

Chloé is working to incorporate sustainability into its operations and management routines, with substantial efforts to align its business practices with social and environmental goals. However, ongoing evaluation and rigorous implementation will be critical to determining whether these efforts are sufficient to achieve long-term sustainability impact. Quantifiable targets, like their greenhouse gas reduction goals, including Scope 3 emissions reporting, can be a step in the right direction, but the true measure of success will be in their consistent delivery and broader industry influence.

The seriousness of the effort, its integration into routine operations management, and its consistency with the firm's history and culture are evident in an excellent November 2022 interview of Chloé CEO Riccardo Bellini by Christopher Marquis in *Forbes*. In the article, CEO Bellini notes:

> Our journey toward creating a purpose-driven business model has been an incredible learning process. When we started, we first looked at our carbon footprint and learned that 58 percent of our impact was from raw materials. Distribution and our operation of

> stores were also contributors to our total footprint. . . . We started to really look at our materials. Throughout our thinking process, we decided that 80 percent of our problems could be solved at the design table. When it comes to materials, it's incredible how easily you can embrace ones that have always been present in the industry. Natural materials like linen and hemp, for example, are especially low impact. So before looking at any big innovations on the market, we made a commitment to shift toward low-impact materials: What made up 10 percent of our materials, we would aim to make up 90 percent by 2025. Next we looked at the more high-impact materials we had been heavily using and began to think of ways to tackle that. Cashmere, for example, has a very high impact, so we started to look for recycled sources. Leather is another very important high-impact material. We knew we had to consider where the leather is coming from, and . . . we also looked to alternative leathers, but that's an ongoing search as there is no real alternative to leather that doesn't open up more issues. Vegan leathers, for example, are mostly made up of plastic- and fossil-fuel-based materials. We have also invested a lot of time in the innovation of circular materials. To decrease the production of new materials and to avoid excess waste of our recycled materials, we began to cycle excess fabric into leftover materials that we could actually use to re-create new designs. When it comes to material innovation, there is going to be a lot said about circular material over the next few years.[25]

This is an impressive demonstration of the degree to which the basic operations of the company have come to consider environmental impacts. At Chloé, this begins with design and the procurement of materials and extends throughout the production process. As with Apple, the centrality of sustainability metrics is clear as the CEO discusses the relationship of design to environmental impact. The interview is remarkable evidence of what must be termed a paradigm shift in management's understanding of how the fashion world works. Clearly, the demand for sustainability, even in luxury goods, is coming from customers, but as with our other case studies, it is equally obvious that the views and values of workers and management are also a critical element of this transition. The CEO's views are also reflected by Chloé's chief designer, Gabriela Hearst. In a March 2023 piece in the *Guardian*, Jess Cartner-Morely interviewed Hearst and reported that:

> The real passion of Gabriela Hearst, the creative director of the Parisian house of Chloé, is sustainability, not fashion. But she works in a luxury business where clothes and handbags pay bills and salaries. Can she balance the books between the environmental and business bottom lines? It is this question, rather than what length skirts should be this season, that keeps Hearst up at night. "I never think about trends. If I hit a trend it's a complete accident. I inherited my mum's wardrobe, my daughters take their denim from me. Quality is everything. People ask why my clothes cost so much. It is because the fabric and construction will last your lifetime and beyond."[26]

Chloé's tradition was pathbreaking from its start in 1952, begun by Gaby Aghion, an Egyptian Jewish woman, who named the brand for a friend rather than the more common practice of naming it for oneself. Still, the fashion business is the very definition of conspicuous consumption, and it is engaged in more than providing the basic human need of clothing. For some critics, sustainable fashion is an oxymoron because it is pure luxury. However, because it will continue in one form or another and fulfills a creative and cultural function, it is certainly positive that this company has integrated sustainability into its operations.

BlackRock

Laurence Fink, the chairman and CEO of BlackRock, was an early proponent of ESG investment and recognized and argued for the importance of sustainability finance. In Fink's 2021 letter to CEOs, he observed:

> In January of last year, I wrote that climate risk is investment risk. I said then that as markets started to price climate risk into the value

> of securities, it would spark a fundamental reallocation of capital. Then the pandemic took hold—and in March, the conventional wisdom was the crisis would divert attention from climate. But just the opposite took place, and the reallocation of capital accelerated even faster than I anticipated. From January through November 2020, investors in mutual funds and ETFs invested $288 billion globally in sustainable assets, a 96 percent increase over the whole of 2019. I believe that this is the beginning of a long but rapidly accelerating transition—one that will unfold over many years and reshape asset prices of every type. We know that climate risk is investment risk. But we also believe the climate transition presents a historic investment opportunity.[27]

However, by 2024, responding to the political attack on "woke management," Fink dropped explicit references to ESG while rebranding sustainability investment as "transition investment." In a *Wall Street Journal* piece published in March 2024, Jack Pitcher and Amrith Ramkumar observed:

> Climate investing is booming at BlackRock.[28] Just don't call it ESG. After crusading for years[29] for investment funds and companies to take into account environmental, social and governance factors, Larry Fink has purged the letters from his vocabulary. He attempted to use BlackRock's clout as the steward for millions of investors to prod companies toward climate-friendly policies and press them to disclose the social effects of their businesses. He long argued that the world's largest asset manager and its peers could make money and make the world a better place at the same time. Fast forward to 2024, and the chief executive has stopped mentioning the acronym in public letters and comments. He retreated after a backlash from conservative pundits against "woke capitalism" made the term politically toxic. Furthermore, he faced criticism,[30] even in the finance industry, from people who said he was moralizing, playing God and stepping beyond BlackRock's fiduciary duty to maximize financial returns for clients. BlackRock is still wagering that fighting climate change will be a generational investment opportunity—but

> the company is no longer pushing for changes in corporate behavior, talking about hard-to-quantify social issues or actively promoting ESG investing criteria. Instead, it is directing billions of client dollars toward infrastructure projects that will help speed the transition from fossil fuels.[31]

In our view, this is a retreat from ideological ESG as an *end* and instead a shift in focus on green infrastructure investment as a *means*. BlackRock is integrating sustainability into the *process* of routine management and removing it as a goal. However, abandoning the nonenvironmental elements of sustainability would be a mistake. Although BlackRock is not issuing communiques about these issues, it appears to continue to utilize sustainability metrics and integrate them into routine management.

BlackRock has tried to integrate sustainability into its operations, embedding it into both investment strategies and internal management practices. With $800 billion invested in sustainable businesses and a commitment to reaching net-zero carbon emissions by 2050, the company demonstrates a strong alignment between its strategic goals and sustainability initiatives. This integration is further reflected in their divestment from nonsustainable sectors such as thermal coal and in their extensive sustainability reporting, which adheres to standards like GRI, SASB, and TCFD.

However, although BlackRock's sustainability goals are comprehensive, there are areas where progress is less transparent. The lack of explicit sustainability metrics in employee performance reviews and management compensation suggests that sustainability may not be fully embedded into every aspect of the company's operations. Additionally, the absence of detailed information on water sustainability practices and department-wide sustainability funding indicates potential gaps in their otherwise robust approach.

However, overall, BlackRock's sustainability efforts are emblematic of a firm that has begun to integrate these principles into its core operations. There is room for further enhancement, particularly in ensuring that sustainability metrics are uniformly applied across all levels of the organization and fully integrated into compensation structures. Moreover, the absence of a dedicated sustainability department and budget may indicate that sustainability, once a key part of BlackRock's public-facing strategy, might not be as deeply ingrained in its internal operations as it appears. Monitoring Scope 1, 2, and 3 emissions, committing to their reduction, and aligning employee incentives with sustainability goals could further solidify their leadership.

As an investment firm rather than an operating organization, BlackRock is the classic service sector finance organization whose greatest influence is in how it directs capital. In that respect, it needs to be analyzed more for its influence on capital formation than for its own operations. Despite the retreat from ESG ideology, its pivot into green infrastructure investment can be seen as a significant case of the integration of sustainability metrics into routine management and into the organization's business plan. Greenhouse gas reduction is connected to the modernization of the energy system. In that sense, the mitigation of climate change is a positive by-product of a lower cost, more reliable energy system. Having BlackRock's tremendous financial power aligned with the decarbonization transition is more significant than any CEO letter Mr. Fink could ever publish.

The changes we witnessed in the investment community in 2023 and 2024 saw a move away from "ESG"-identified funds to renewable energy infrastructure projects. According, once again, to the *Wall Street Journal*'s Jack Pitcher and Amrith Ramkumar:

> Another reason the ESG movement failed to catch on was because the funds struggled to outpace the broader market and show that they actually benefited the planet. Investors pulled about $13 billion, or roughly 4 percent of assets, from publicly traded ESG funds last year, according to Morningstar.[32] BlackRock's offering of mostly index-tracking ESG funds posted inflows. Investors poured about $75 billion into private renewable-energy and broad energy-sector investment funds over the same period. The funds have raised nearly $500 billion in the past five years and dwarfed the amount raised for traditional fossil-fuel funds, figures from Preqin show. Total global

> investment in energy transition hit about $1.8 trillion last year, a roughly 17 percent increase from 2022, according to data provider BloombergNEF.[33]

It is important to acknowledge and understand the importance of BlackRock's leadership role in this maturing world of sustainability finance. The measures of renewable energy investment have become part of the language of infrastructure investment. The financial opportunities present in this sector are the single most significant factors driving the decarbonization of the world economy, quite possibly leading to the mitigation of climate change.

CONCLUSION

This chapter reviewed the integration and routinization of sustainability metrics into organizational operations and business plans. This is a process well underway and, in many ways, one that resembles prior shifts in organizational management, including the rise of financial management beginning in the 1930s, informational management in the 1960s and 1970s, and global trade and supply chains late in the twentieth century. Management continues to evolve as the economy becomes more complex and as technologies like computing, communication, transportation, and renewable energy evolve. We will see more of this in the next several decades as sustainability management becomes as routinized as accounting and financial management.

5

ENVIRONMENT, DEI, TRANSPARENT ORGANIZATIONAL GOVERNANCE, AND COMMUNITY IMPACT

Ideology and Management Competence

This chapter addresses the broadened conceptualization of sustainability, going beyond environmental sustainability to incorporate aspects of diversity, equity, transparent governance, and an organization's community impact. Although many critics of sustainability consider it to be ideological and not related to organizational management, this chapter continues to build the management case for this broader definition of sustainability and considers its inclusion central to competent and effective management. Environmental sustainability remains a critical element of sustainability management, but there is a strong case for these nonphysical dimensions of sustainability as well.

As noted earlier, in a global, brain-based economy, an organization that reflects non-talent-related biases when hiring and promoting staff reduces its talent pool and ability to compete. Homogeneity of senior management and organizational governance eliminates multiple perspectives and life experiences from the management process. This increases the probability of flawed strategy and decision-making.

Finally, an organization that ignores its impact on its host community runs the risk of generating political opposition to expansion plans and difficulty in recruiting key staff. This chapter makes the case that more mindful and careful management tends to be more effective and competent management. An organization that abuses its host community will typically generate unpredictable and negative responses. A well-managed organization will work to avoid negative environmental and community impacts.[1]

THE DEFINITION OF SUSTAINABILITY IS EVOLVING

In the twenty-first century, the definition of sustainability includes environmental factors, resource management, life expectancy, and lifestyle. We trace the concept of sustainability back to the nineteenth century and Henry George, who wrote about the notion of "Spaceship Earth."[2] This idea evolved into "sustainable development" in the Brundtland Report of 1987. The report defined sustainable development as "development that meets the needs of the present generations without compromising the ability of future generations to meet their own needs."[3]

According to Herman Daly, the former chief economist of the World Bank, a sustainable society needs to meet three straightforward conditions. First, renewable resources, such as fish stocks, oil, and groundwater, should be extracted at a rate not exceeding the natural regeneration capacity. Second, nonrenewable resources, including minerals and fossil fuels, ought to be consumed no faster than renewable substitutes can be developed and implemented. And third, pollution and waste emissions must not exceed the natural systems' capacity to absorb, recycle, or neutralize them.[4]

Although this framework primarily addresses environmental sustainability, its deeper integration into public consciousness fosters a broader and deeper understanding of sustainability in everyday life. As individuals recognize the interconnectedness of ecological development with social, economic, and cultural dimensions, diverse interpretations and applications of sustainability principles across various sectors and communities emerge. This shift encourages holistic approaches that address not only environmental concerns but also social equity, economic empowerment, and quality of life, thus enriching the overall discourse on sustainable development.

THE TRIPLE BOTTOM LINE

As we discussed in chapter 3 of this book, the Triple Bottom Line (TBL) is a sustainability-related concept based on three fundamental pillars: profit, people, and planet.[5] This model emphasizes that sustainable success should not be measured solely by financial profitability but by a balanced consideration of social well-being and environmental governance.

TBL expands the environmental agenda by integrating economic growth and societal development. Although some view sustainability primarily through the lens of environmental or social aspects, TBL offers a more comprehensive, macroscopic perspective that encompasses the interconnected relationships between society, the environment, and the economy. This framework provides a foundational understanding that informs and shapes more detailed models of sustainability, promoting a holistic approach to sustainable development.

UNITED NATIONS GLOBAL COMPACT

The United Nations Global Compact (UNGC) was proposed in 2000 by the then-United Nations secretary general Kofi Annan to address the economic, social, and environmental issues arising from the process of globalization. UNGC encompasses four structures—human rights, labor, environment, and anticorruption[6]—and was discussed in chapter 3 as a framework to guide companies to implement Sustainable Development Goals at the corporate level. In the realm of human rights, it establishes two fundamental principles: first, businesses should support and respect the protection of internationally recognized human rights, and second, they should ensure that they are not complicit in human rights abuses. As a voluntary regulatory program, it has obvious limitations, but it does have over 13,000 committed organizations, over 9,000 of which are corporations spanning 170 countries.[7]

Regarding labor rights, the principles include upholding the freedom of association and recognizing the right to collective bargaining, eliminating all forms of forced and compulsory labor, abolishing child labor, and eradicating discrimination in employment and occupation. When considering environmental responsibility, the UNGC emphasizes that businesses should adopt a precautionary approach to environmental challenges, undertake initiatives to promote greater environmental responsibility, and encourage the development and dissemination of environmentally friendly technologies. For anticorruption, the principles commit businesses to actively combat corruption in all its forms, including extortion and bribery.

A prime example of how the UNGC works in advancing sustainable development is the Global Africa Business Initiative (GABI), which promotes Africa as a premier destination for business, trade, and investment. Cross-sector partnerships leverage large investments from private companies, development banks, governments, social sector organizations, and philanthropies.

The goals of the UNGC and the concept of the TBL are closely related yet distinct in their focus and application. The TBL emphasizes the importance of balancing people (social), planet (environmental), and profit (economic) considerations in business practices. It serves as a foundational framework for measuring sustainability, encouraging businesses to look beyond financial profits to include their social and environmental impact. The UNGC provides specific principles and guidelines for corporate responsibility across these four pillars and offers a broader conceptual framework that encourages holistic evaluation of business performance. The principles outlined in the UNGC can be viewed as practical applications of the TBL philosophy, translating its ideals into actionable commitments for businesses.

UNITED NATIONS MILLENNIUM DEVELOPMENT GOALS

As noted in chapter 3, the Millennium Development Goals (MDGs) are eight development goals initiated by the United Nations for the period from 2000 to 2015 aimed at addressing global poverty, including eradicating extreme poverty and hunger; achieving universal primary education; promoting gender equality; reducing child mortality; improving maternal health; combating HIV/AIDS, malaria, and other diseases; ensuring environmental sustainability; and fostering global partnerships for development.[8]

Although the MDGs focus more on social development goals such as health, education, and gender equality, they also represent an extension of the principles underlying the TBL framework. Because the TBL highlights the balance between economic, social, and environmental pillars, it lays the groundwork for a more structured approach to sustainable development by demonstrating the interconnectedness of these three areas. The UNGC further complemented this framework by establishing specific guidelines for responsible business practices across human rights, labor, environment, and anticorruption. The MDGs, then, expanded on the TBL and UNGC by emphasizing specific social and human development targets and still incorporated environmental sustainability.

UNITED NATIONS 2030 SUSTAINABLE DEVELOPMENT GOALS

As noted earlier, the Sustainable Development Goals encompass the core principles of the MDGs, including ending poverty, improving health and education, and reducing inequality. They also broadened the agenda by incorporating goals aimed at spurring economic growth, addressing climate change, and safeguarding the planet's natural resources, including oceans and forests. The Sustainable Development Goals represent a shift from a primary focus on human development to a more holistic approach that emphasizes the integration of human well-being with the environment, economic systems, and future sustainability. This expanded scope highlights the need to balance human progress with the protection and preservation of the planet for future generations.

DEFINING AND MEASURING SUSTAINABILITY BEYOND ENVIRONMENTAL INDICES

The TBL, UNGC, MDGs, and Sustainable Development Goals differ in specific definitions and standards, but their core principles are fundamentally aligned in their pursuit of a more equitable and sustainable world. Based on these interrelated concepts and their developmental track, sustainability can be defined as the integration of environmental governance, social equity, and economic viability. It requires organizations to meet present and future needs while minimizing harm to communities and the environment. It also enhances resilience through effective management that fosters diversity and the transparency of organizational decision-making.

From our perspective, sustainability is a multifactored concept that concentrates on environmental issues but has evolved to encompass dimensions of diversity, equity, transparent governance, and community impact. This comprehensive understanding of sustainability highlights its relevance across various sectors of society and emphasizes the necessity for organizations to adopt a holistic approach that aligns their operational strategies with broader societal goals. We recognize that these lofty goals seem disconnected from hard-headed and profit-focused organizational management. Nevertheless, it is our view that on a more crowded, interconnected, and observed planet, mindfulness about the organization's impact on people and the planet and awareness of the impact of people and the planet on the organization now compose a central element of management effectiveness.

Although there are many definitions and principles of sustainability, many of them focus on the environmental factors. We retain that focus, but our research has identified three major additional dimensions of *organizational* sustainability—the internal operation of the organization, the organization's impact on its host community, and its overall impact on global well-being. The organizational dimension encompasses internal practices and policies that promote ethical behavior, diversity, equitable treatment of employees, and future organizational development. This includes many aspects such as their vision, mission and values, strategic plan, and commitment to innovation and continuous improvement. For the organization's sustainability dimension, the focus is on fostering an organizational culture that prioritizes employee well-being, encourages collaboration, and embraces inclusivity and overall equity. It also includes transparency of organizational governance, particularly to investors providing capital to the organization.

The community dimension emphasizes the organization's social impact, including its relationship with the local community and its people, culture, and economy. Sustainable organizations actively engage their surrounding communities, addressing social issues, supporting local initiatives and the underprivileged, encouraging growth, and fostering economic development. This engagement enhances the organization's reputation and deepens its connection to the community. Often referred to as corporate social responsibility, these activities enhance corporate image and support regional growth and well-being.

The societal dimension reflects the broader social responsibilities and impact of organizations, emphasizing the importance of building a diverse and inclusive society. This level of impact can enhance social welfare and promote sustainable development at a macro level. As an organization takes on a social responsibility initiative, it should constantly reflect on whether its impact is having the desired result or not. As an organization's impact increases, it must include self-compliance and reflection mechanisms on integrity, anticorruption, and negative external impacts.

THE CHALLENGE OF MEASURING A BROADER CONCEPT OF SUSTAINABILITY

Once we have clarified the definition of the environmental and nonenvironmental elements of organizational sustainability, the next step is to determine how can we achieve it and measure it and the difficulties and issues in doing so. It is relatively straightforward (and there is some consensus) on how to measure environmental sustainability. Organizations assess their environmental performance through indicators such as energy consumption, carbon footprint, waste management, resource efficiency, and so on.[9] These indicators are incorporated into recognized frameworks like the Global Reporting Initiative (GRI) and Carbon Disclosure Project (CDP)—which we detail elsewhere in the book—providing somewhat standardized methods for tracking sustainability efforts.

In terms of resource utilization, companies can promote circular economy principles, such as the "3R" approach—Reduce, Reuse, and Recycle—to maximize resource efficiency and minimize waste.[10] Specifically, companies can focus on energy efficiency and emission reduction by adopting energy-saving technologies, optimizing production processes, and enhancing equipment efficiency.

Additionally, investing in environmental innovation plays a crucial role in developing sustainable solutions,[11] such as clean production technologies and low-carbon products, which further improve environmental performance. Green supply chain management allows companies to extend sustainability beyond internal operations.[12] Organizations can select environmentally friendly raw materials, optimize logistics, collaborate with suppliers, and contractually require vendors to reduce environmental impact. Organizations can shift toward renewable energy sources to reduce reliance on fossil fuels and lower their carbon footprint, and firms can cultivate a green supply chain that fosters collective environmental responsibility.

There is extensive research on the relationship between organizational culture and its impact on employee performance and productivity. As the postpandemic workplace evolves, the expectations and satisfaction of employees are also in a continuous process of change. In response, organizational culture is adjusting in response to these dynamic shifts and, to some degree, seeking to respond to the expanding demands for employee well-being, engagement, and satisfaction, all the while striving to become sustainable.[13] At the same time, there are political and ideological pressures for and against the effective management of diversity, equity, and inclusion

(DEI), as many organizations still struggle to fully integrate these principles into their core operations.

Sustainable development provides a viable framework for addressing the persistent issue of workplace bias. Numerous studies have highlighted racial and gender disparities within organizations, particularly in high-status positions.[14] Although white women, women of color, and men of color have made notable progress in entering craft, managerial, and professional roles since the 1960s, they continue to be underrepresented, especially when compared to their white male counterparts.[15] These disparities underscore the need for inclusive organizational practices as part of broader sustainability efforts. Again, we are not arguing for quotas and non-merit-based hiring practices. Rather, we are identifying a long-term issue that is far from being resolved.

In organizations, categorical distinctions and symbolic boundaries are frequently established based on social status indicators such as gender, race, ethnicity, class, and age, as well as the nature of work, whether it be manual labor, beauty care, or executive decision-making.[16] Women and people of color are often channeled into roles characterized by lower pay, diminished status, and limited autonomy.[17] These groups frequently encounter "glass ceilings," which are discriminatory barriers that obstruct their progression to senior leadership positions within organizations.[18]

Although progress toward fairness is happening, these conditions in the workplace are both reflective of and reinforce symbolic boundaries that separate men from women, white individuals from people of color, and the elderly from the young.[19] Even when women and people of color ascend to higher positions, they frequently report lacking informal social power, such as the sense of security that their white male counterparts often take for granted. These boundaries are deeply embedded within the "practices of division" that characterize some workplace dynamics.[20]

DEI is not merely an issue of race, ethnicity, or gender but also involves a wide variety of characteristics, including disabilities. Some major organizations, such as Microsoft, have taken steps that provide some examples of what might be possible and sustainable.

Microsoft states that it has shaped its organizational culture to prioritize diversity and inclusion, particularly with a focus on integrating individuals with intellectual and developmental disabilities (I/DD) into its workforce. Through its Real Estate and Facilities vendor ecosystem, Microsoft supports workers with I/DD by ensuring they receive equitable wages and benefits from their employers. These employees are embedded into over thirty distinct roles, such as café ambassador, shuttle fueler, warehouse technician, reception assistant, and similar titles,[21] fostering a work environment where individuals of all abilities can collaborate and contribute to the corporation.

Further advancing its commitment to inclusivity, Microsoft has taken steps to ensure that its hiring process for individuals with disabilities is accessible. The company offers accommodations upfront, tailoring the interview process to include fewer interviews per day, longer breaks, and interactive discussions to alleviate barriers that may hinder a candidate's success.[22] This initiative has helped create a more equitable and supportive interview experience, ensuring that candidates with disabilities can compete for full-time positions on a level playing field, which enriches the organizational culture and contributes to broader societal progress, in turn making the company culture much more sustainable.

Microsoft's intention toward equity extends to gender and racial representation at the highest levels of its corporate structure. As of 2024, Microsoft's board of directors is one of the most diverse in the technology industry, with women and ethnic minorities holding nine out of twelve board positions.[23] Microsoft is seeking to illustrate its commitment to diversity in leadership and perhaps project a broader example of sustainable, inclusive growth in the corporate sector. Through a wide array of diversity initiatives, Microsoft hopes to mitigate inequity in its workforce and illustrate how inclusivity and equity are integral to achieving sustainable organizational development. Only the passage of time will tell whether removing systemic barriers and fostering an inclusive culture make Microsoft a leader in promoting long-term social and economic sustainability aligned with its broader Sustainable Development Goals. Given the technical expertise long demonstrated by Microsoft, it is safe to assume that issues of merit continue to be factored into all hiring and promotion actions.

A much less optimistic picture of the prospects for DEI initiatives in the workplace emerges from a study of the University of Michigan's decade of effort to build one of the largest and most comprehensive DEI programs of any public university in the United States. A detailed examination by the *New York Times* concluded that the decade-long effort by the university spent nearly $250 million, created 241 related job titles, required every unit to have a DEI plan, and yet struggled to achieve its central goals and set off a series of unintended consequences.[24] Among the more striking results to date is that the percentage of Black students remained at 5 percent in a state that is 14 percent African American, even as overall enrollment rose. Surveys also indicated that over that time span, students and faculty reported a less positive campus climate and less of a sense of belonging.

Since 2015, complaints of sex- or gender-based misconduct increased from 200 to over 500 in 2023, and complaints regarding race, religion, or national origin rose from less than 110 to nearly 400 on the Michigan campus. The *New York Times* also reported that after the Hamas October 7, 2023, attacks on Israel, the US Department of Education found that the university had "systematically mishandled 67 complaints of harassment or discrimination" and issued findings in just one case.[25] Although neither the Microsoft nor the Michigan case is definitive, we believe they make the case for measurement that is used to reinforce the effectiveness of the program or provide the basis for modification or, if warranted, abandonment of the initiative.

Professors Paul Brest and Emily J. Levine argue that a new approach is needed, at least for the university and nonprofit sector, based on pluralism. They argue that many DEI programs are based on online or standardized training with one message—the world is filled with pervasive discrimination. People should embrace their own identities, values, and experiences while acknowledging differences with others and looking together for common ground. Programs need to focus on building a wide sense of belonging and engagement among diverse groups.[26] They have yet to suggest how we can measure the success of this approach. The measurement task is exacerbated by the complexity of diversity goals. From a management perspective, the goal for diversity is not demographic representation but diversity of lived experiences. That is not as easy to measure as a person's gender or race. The goal is to create a positive, welcoming environment, not an environment that divides people based on explicit or implicit distinctions.

THE IMPORTANCE OF ORGANIZATIONAL IMPACT ON THE COMMUNITY

The primary responsibility of most business corporations is generally thought of as the generation of profit. Over time and particularly beginning in the second half of the twentieth century, a broader responsibility for the creation of shared value has emerged, widely known as corporate social responsibility (CSR).[27] CSR is integral to achieving organizational sustainability.[28] Traditionally, CSR was strongly associated with philanthropy, but it has since expanded to focus on the broader relationship between business and society, emphasizing the role of corporations in addressing social challenges.[29] Today, CSR is also referred to as corporate responsibility, corporate citizenship, responsible business, or corporate social opportunity, and it encompasses a corporation's accountability for the social and environmental impacts of its activities on stakeholders, such as customers, suppliers, employees, shareholders, communities, and the broader environment.[30]

Modern CSR refers to the strategic practices that corporations or firms adopt to conduct business in an ethical and socially responsible manner. CSR encompasses a wide range of activities, including partnerships with local communities; socially responsible investments; fostering strong relationships with employees, customers, and their families; and initiatives aimed at environmental conservation and sustainability. At a higher level, CSR's community dimension emphasizes the social, environmental, and economic impacts of corporate actions on local communities. We will also explore the role of businesses in society, the stakeholder approach, and the concept of the social contract.

The interactive relationship between business and society is crucial because CSR encompasses the obligation of businesses to consider the broader social impact of their business decisions and actions, considering their social power and influence in the community. One measure of CSR is the perceived importance of economic dynamism within society, which underscores the role that businesses play in contributing to economic growth and political stability.[31] This includes creating jobs, fostering innovation, and supporting local economies through responsible business practices. Additionally, CSR emphasizes the importance of companies recognizing their responsibilities toward the entire social system rather than just their own benefit.[32] Business leaders should evaluate how their choices impact not only their organizations but also the communities and environments in which they operate. This is not undertaken because businesses are altruistic because, by design, they are not. Corporations are profit-seeking entities designed to increase profit, market share, and return on equity. To reiterate, we are simply maintaining that on a more crowded and economically interconnected planet, organizations cannot see themselves as isolated from their physical, cultural, and economic environments. If management ignores the world around the organization, they will set in motion unanticipated negative impacts that can impair organizational effectiveness. Therefore, an understanding of the impact of the organization on its environment is simply a core concept of competent, effective management.

The stakeholder approach is an important strategy for enhancing corporate management effectiveness and organizational sustainability. A business operates in an interconnected web of diverse interests, where the processes of self-creation and community creation occur interdependently.[33] Within this framework, the stakeholder approach combines both integrative and ethical theories.

The integrative aspect focuses on harmonizing social demands with business objectives, whereas the ethical dimension underscores the moral obligations of businesses to engage in practices that contribute to a just, equitable, and eventually sustainable society. Again, organizations do not pursue these goals due to altruism or an ideology of "doing good" but out of a broader and enlightened sense of self-interest. For example, by identifying different categories of community, a firm can pinpoint areas and demographics they could focus on, managing relationships with the firm and the community. This mutual perspective reinforces the notion that the social responsibilities of business leaders should reflect the extent of their social power and influence.[34]

A social contract framework provides a macro-level understanding of the relationship between corporations and society. It acts as the foundation for analyzing how businesses engage with broader social structures and their obligations within them. CSR is based on the belief that corporations derive their legitimacy and sustainability from societal acceptance. CSR is more than a set of voluntary good deeds; it is a response to the ethical expectations embedded in the social contract between businesses and the communities in which they operate.[35] The social contract framework requires businesses to align their actions with the values and norms of society, including respect of human rights, labor rights, environmental stewardship, fairness, and antidiscrimination. The social contract framework requires that business actions reflect a commitment to a common good. This is done because the alternative—acting in either ignorance of the community or in active opposition to community interests—risks political and consumer blowback and damage to a company's brand. *This does not mean that the "common good" is easily defined or easily measured.* At several points in this work, we have introduced a variety of these organizational sustainability frameworks, but we present their sheer number and introduce their conceptual murkiness to provide the reader with a deeper understanding of the complexity of measuring and managing the nonenvironmental dimensions of sustainability.

Despite this difficulty, we can provide examples of mindful and responsible behavior to enhance the operational meaning of these concepts. The Jasan Group, a public company in China, is an organization that exemplifies a strong commitment to CSR and a broad array of sustainability principles.[36] Despite operating in a traditional textile industry often associated with environmental challenges, Jasan has implemented numerous eco-friendly initiatives. The company actively monitors and reduces water consumption, minimizes wastewater discharge, and utilizes renewable energy sources such as solar power to decrease carbon emissions.

Moreover, Jasan prioritizes employee well-being by providing family housing and childcare facilities, which offers social and economic stability for its workforce. It also supports women's empowerment through programs like Personal Advancement and Career Enhancement (PACE), fostering women's personal development and career growth. To enhance long-term development and sustainability, Jasan collaborates with educational institutions to create a pipeline of skilled workers. Through all these efforts, Jasan Group has enhanced its operational performance in part due to the impact of its commitment to CSR and sustainable development.

Quantifying CSR remains a complex challenge.[37] How well businesses fulfill their social responsibilities is difficult to measure, given the complex and long-term characteristics of social impact. Traditional metrics often focus on financial performance or compliance with regulations, but they may not adequately capture the broader societal benefits or harms associated with business activities. Therefore, developing comprehensive frameworks that assess both the qualitative and quantitative aspects of CSR, as we discussed in chapter 1, is essential for understanding its true impact on society and sustainability. We assume that these metrics will be situational and will need to be adjusted to culture and other aspects of local conditions. We do not underestimate the difficulty of this measurement task.

THE IMPORTANCE OF ORGANIZATIONAL IMPACT ON SOCIETY

First, it is unrealistic to require every organization and every firm to achieve comprehensive sustainability. True sustainability is a complex and long-term endeavor that may exceed the resources and expertise of smaller organizations or organizations under stress. And some corporations may stay focused only on short-term profit maximization. Although there is no doubt that sustainable development will offer long-term benefits for employees, organizations, communities, and society at large, it is not easily attainable for all firms. Although the importance of CSR has gained considerable attention in recent years, the reality is that many organizations will continue to prioritize immediate financial gains over sustainable practices.

For organizations committed to long-term success, it is essential to embed sustainability into the organizational culture and strategic goals. This involves not only complying with external regulations but also internalizing sustainability as a core organizational value. When sustainability is deeply integrated into the company's mission, culture, and strategic objectives, it fosters a unified approach where every employee is aligned with and working toward common sustainability goals. It also changes not only their operational practices but also the mindset and behaviors of their workforce. Sustainability helps create a collective sense of purpose that transcends individual roles and contributes to the broader aim of achieving social, environmental, and economic sustainability.

Second, it is difficult to establish uniform criteria for nonenvironmental sustainability, as each organization needs to develop its own sustainable development plan according to its actual field and development situation. For example, for polluting enterprises, reducing emissions and greening the environment are the top priorities. These organizations often face regulatory pressures and societal expectations that compel them to adopt practices aimed at minimizing their environmental footprint. Conversely, small and start-up organizations may struggle to allocate resources toward community development initiatives as their focus must be to survive and become profitable. Start-ups often operate with limited budgets and few paid staff, making it difficult to prioritize broader social responsibilities when immediate survival and growth are at stake. Their focus is establishing a viable business model and achieving financial stability, which can overshadow community engagement efforts.

Although the need for sustainability is widely recognized, the pathways to achieving it are diverse and context dependent. Organizations must navigate their specific challenges and opportunities to develop effective sustainability plans that align with their operational realities and the expectations of their stakeholders, particularly investors and customers. This tailored approach reflects the unique circumstances of the organization, such as its industry, size, market conditions, and social or regulatory pressures. The complexity of this process makes it difficult to establish standardized measures of success, as sustainability initiatives should be both adaptable and context specific, evolving in response to internal and external forces.

Third, it's not easy to achieve long-term, nonenvironmentally sustainable development. Such an approach requires substantial investments of both time and financial resources. Organizations pursuing nonenvironmental sustainability must often forgo some immediate profits in favor of long-term benefits, necessitating a commitment to invest in various initiatives, such as constructing facilities like apartments, gyms, and canteens for employees, as well as contributing to welfare programs and supporting vulnerable populations in need. These investments not only demand considerable financial outlays but also require a prolonged timeframe before yielding positive returns.

The delay in receiving tangible benefits can pose operational challenges within organizations, particularly in maintaining stakeholder engagement and justifying the initial expenditures. In addition, the complexity of managing these investments raises concerns regarding governance and accountability, particularly with respect to preventing corruption and ensuring that resources are allocated effectively.

Evaluating the effectiveness of such initiatives goes beyond traditional metrics, demanding new tools and frameworks that can capture social, ethical, and long-term impacts on various stakeholders. Ensuring ethical governance and preventing corruption within the entity becomes crucial because mismanagement or unethical practices could undermine the credibility and effectiveness of sustainability efforts. Balancing all these challenges requires long-term vision, strong leadership, and a deep integration of sustainability principles into the organization's culture and operations.

To achieve environmental sustainability, collaboration between the public and private sectors is often required. The development of renewable resource-based technologies relies on long-term funding from the government for basic scientific research. The government is crucial in enforcing sustainability regulations and environmental laws, acting as an environmental watchdog. Finally, the government must establish decarbonization targets and leverage regulatory and tax powers to meet these objectives.[38] During the second Trump administration, we saw many of these tasks being abandoned by the federal government but being absorbed by state and local governments. Corporations committed to environmental sustainability continue to pursue these commitments and are not affected by a diminished federal role. Each sector has distinct responsibilities, so effective collaboration and cooperation are vital for success.

WHY A BROADER DEFINITION OF SUSTAINABILITY IS SO IMPORTANT

Sustainability management is not an ideological position; it is a new and more comprehensive approach to management effectiveness. It includes a concern for efficiency through waste reduction and building a workforce for the long term by treating workers inclusively and with respect. These practices foster innovation through inclusion and a sense of belonging. The organization creates a symbiotic relationship with stakeholders, the community, and society, often through cross-sector partnerships. This reduces political friction and enhances community support while building a brand's reputation. Environmental sustainability is an essential part of sustainability management, but the nonphysical dimensions of sustainability discussed in this chapter are critical for organizational well-being.

Organizations that seek to maximize their positive impact on their host community will build political and public support for their continuing success and expansion locally. Firms that build a diverse workforce, invest in professional development, and pay a living wage with benefits will tend to achieve sustainable success. A well-managed organization will recognize that its contribution to building a healthy society will not only survive but will grow and prosper in the long term.

Achieving sustainable development presents numerous challenges, yet it is increasingly recognized as essential for individuals, organizations, and society. The complexities involved in implementing and measuring sustainable practices require significant commitment and resources, which will cost time, money, and energy. However, the pursuit of sustainability is not merely a passing trend but a fundamental requirement for the long-term viability of businesses and communities. As global expectations shift toward more responsible and ethical practices, the pressure on organizations to integrate sustainability into their operations continues to intensify.

6

MEASUREMENT AND DISCLOSURE OF CARBON AND CLIMATE RISKS

Today, with environmental awareness rising around the globe and climate uncertainty becoming ever more extreme, businesses are increasingly expected to take a close look at their carbon emissions and the climate-related risks they face. It is no longer sufficient that these challenges are just recognized; organizations are called upon to measure, report, and actively manage the risks from the changing climate. This chapter explores the methods organizations can use to measure emissions, as well as the frameworks through which companies disclose the physical and transition risks of climate change. The chapter also discusses the measures organizations adopt to mitigate these risks. We recognize that environmental risk is broader than climate change, but for simplicity's sake and to provide an example of the measurement challenges, this chapter focuses on climate change.

The accounting and reporting of emissions and climate risks would be important not only for compliance with regulatory requirements but also for investor confidence, competitiveness, and operational corporate responsibility. Organizations take various approaches to improve their understanding of and preparedness for climate-related risks through the use of scenario analysis and geospatial mapping, which we discuss in this chapter. Global frameworks, such as the Task Force on Climate-Related Financial

Disclosures (TCFD), set standards for companies to report their emissions data in a consistent and comparable way across industries and geographies.

As we move toward a low-carbon economy, the integration of carbon and climate risk management within core business strategies has changed from an added advantage to a prerequisite for long-term profitability and sustainability. This chapter provides an in-depth review of the main practices and methodologies organizations have adopted to navigate the complex landscape of climate risk assessment and reporting.

METHODOLOGIES FOR CALCULATING CARBON EMISSIONS

Accurate quantification of carbon emissions is a critical step for developing feasible and evidence-based objectives for reduction. Both corporations and governments lack the ability to assess progress, identify areas in need of emission reduction, or modify their approaches without reliable data that will match relevant emissions targets. Successful climate strategies require reliable measurements.

As the list of countries adopting carbon taxes, emissions trading systems, and other regulatory frameworks increases, the accuracy of emissions measurement becomes more relevant for ensuring compliance. Companies operating globally must provide accurate emissions information to avoid fines and other penalties. Beyond that, as climate risk and sustainability increasingly become central issues, investors and other stakeholders rely on transparent emissions data to learn about a company's performance on climate mitigation and adaptation. Through clear and accurate reporting of their emissions, organizations can demonstrate how much they are committed to reducing their carbon footprint in order to achieve, for example, net-zero targets.

From a policy perspective, reliable and timely emissions data underpins climate action and policy development at local, national, and international levels. Policymakers need to have accurate emissions information to formulate climate policies, allocate carbon credits, and design mechanisms such as carbon prices and cap-and-trade systems. Without reliable data, it will not be possible to determine the extent of progress made toward meeting international climate goals.

There are different methodologies to quantify and estimate carbon emissions, through either direct measurement techniques or estimation models. Understanding these methodologies is the first step toward quantifying an organization's carbon footprint and assuring credibility in its sustainability endeavors.

Direct Measurement of Carbon Emissions

Clearly, measuring emissions at the source would be the most accurate approach to measurement. Measuring emissions at the source requires utilizing special instruments at the point where emissions are being released. This direct approach is most used in industries such as power generation and cement production, where emissions are linked to energy use or industrial processes.

One of the most commonly used tools for direct measurement is called the Continuous Emissions Monitoring System (CEMS). It is used in many different facilities, including power generation plants, refineries, and manufacturing sites. These monitoring systems work constantly to determine the levels of emissions, such as carbon dioxide (CO_2), within exhaust stacks or flue gas. CEMS data provides the most accurate tracking of emissions actually occurring at any one point in time and due to any given set of activities. In a power plant, for instance, CEMS can track emissions of CO_2 generated through the burning of fossil fuels. These data can be used to facilitate adjustment in operations that reduce emissions. In cement production, CEMS monitors emissions from both the burning of fossil fuel and the chemical process that transforms limestone into lime. The system captures gas samples and analyzes them using infrared sensors or gas analyzers, which can inform the concentration of CO_2. These readings are then used to calculate total emissions based on the volume and makeup of the gas.[1]

Indirect Measurement and Estimation Models

Although direct CO_2 measurement provides a high level of accuracy, in many cases, it is not practical to implement, particularly in large institutions or industries with diversified and scattered sources of emissions. When that happens, organizations can employ indirect measurement methods, which derive estimates of carbon footprint by examining data related to the organization's operations as well as data on consumption patterns. The indirect measurement methods usually rely on an emission factor–based approach, which makes use of established emission factors that represent the average amount of CO_2 released per unit of activity, whether it is the burning of a specific type of fuel or using a certain amount of electricity. As an example, there are emission factors for the combustion of coal, oil, and natural gas, which are then multiplied by the amount of fuel consumed to estimate total CO_2 emissions.

This is widely adopted for Scope 1 emissions, where direct data on fuel consumption and energy use is available. For Scope 2 emissions, it is common to use national or regional grid emission factors to estimate the carbon emissions from purchased electricity based on the average carbon intensity of the electricity grid. The factor-based approach is a more straightforward method, and it is widely used because it requires no equipment and fewer resources than trying to measure emissions at every source. However, there is a trade-off, which is accuracy. Emission factors represent estimated averages and do not always capture all of the variables that can or may affect emissions, including but not limited to fuel types used and/or technological efficiencies in the process.[2]

When deciding the type of activity to include in the emissions calculations, one usually looks at an input-output table. These tables are based on an analysis of economic activities in an economy that trace the flow of goods and services. For example, by analyzing the use of inputs, such as raw materials and energy by sector and industry, input-output tables allow us to trace the production and consumption of specific goods and services. We can then use the published emission factors to calculate the emissions levels associated with various economic activities. In this fashion, input-output tables play a critical role, especially in the estimation of Scope 3 emissions. Together with the emission factors, these tables can be used to calculate the levels of emissions across entire supply chains, including those of suppliers, customers, and other external entities.

Another widely used methodology to measure emissions is life cycle assessment (LCA), which we have also discussed in other parts of this book. LCA is an analytical tool for measuring the environmental impact of a product or service over its entire life cycle—from raw material extraction to manufacturing, transportation, usage, and end-of-life disposal. LCA calculates the carbon emissions and other environmental impacts associated with each phase of the product's life cycle; thus, the approach generates a more comprehensive view of the product's total environmental footprint, not just during its production phase. For example, an LCA for a smartphone would have to take into account emissions generated from the mining and extracting of raw materials, such as gold and copper for wiring, lithium for its battery, and silicon and various chemicals and metals for its microchip. It would also need to account for the energy consumed during the manufacturing of the various components of the smartphone. This would include the phone's casing, battery, screen, semiconductors, and camera. In addition, the total carbon footprint would need to include emissions generated from transportation, both during production and assembly, when all the parts produced need to be shipped to the assembly line, and when transporting the phones to the consumers and retail stores around the globe. Finally, LCA calculates emissions related to the phone's use by the customer and its disposal or recycling. LCA can also be helpful to assess Scope 3 emissions because companies can use LCA to measure the indirect emissions associated with their products' entire life cycle, from supplier to end user, which are parts of the product's value chain.

Remote Sensing and Satellite Monitoring

Another innovative approach in measuring carbon emissions, particularly on a large scale, is the use of remote sensing and satellite monitoring. Remote sensing uses satellite imagery or airborne sensors to collect data on atmospheric levels of CO_2 and other greenhouse gases. The use of remote sensing to monitor emissions is increasing because some emission sources are difficult to observe directly or comprehensively, such as deforestation, large-scale industrial operations, and extraction of fossil fuels.

In addition, some satellites are equipped with sensors capable of measuring infrared radiation that can then detect the presence of CO_2 in the atmosphere. Researchers can use these satellites to measure emissions for extensive areas. For example, NASA's OCO-2 (Orbiting Carbon Observatory-2) and the European Space Agency's Sentinel-5P satellites are capable of gathering high-resolution data on CO_2 concentrations around the globe.[3] This type of large-scale emissions data is useful for monitoring the trends in carbon emissions and for cross-checking data reported by countries or companies. Thus, remote sensing technologies are useful tools in estimating emissions from hard-to-reach areas like forests and in monitoring overall compliance with international climate agreements. However, although remote sensing is capable of providing global information on atmospheric CO_2 concentrations, it lacks the resolution needed to identify specific sources of emissions at an organizational or facility level.

Challenges and Limitations of Carbon Emission Measurement

Despite the large number of measurement techniques at our disposal, there are still significant challenges in either directly measuring carbon emissions or indirectly estimating them reliably at a large level. For example, indirect emissions, such as those measured for Scope 3 purposes, occur throughout the supply chain, and they are particularly difficult to measure for a variety of reasons. First is the availability and reliability of data. Organizations often depend on their suppliers to provide reliable data on emissions, which in many cases suppliers don't have. Even when suppliers provide data, the data can be incomplete, inconsistent, or inaccurate. This problem is further compounded by a lack of standardization in reporting, and there may be limited verification performed across supply chain companies. All of these factors can lead to ambiguity and the potential for underreporting (or overreporting) emission levels. We hope more and more organizations will start to contract with their suppliers to contractually provide reports of specific environmental measures, with financial penalties imposed if reports are not provided or are inaccurate.

A further challenge arises from the complexity of emission factors. Normally, emission factors are based on average values and are used to calculate emissions based on activity data such as fuel consumption or energy use. However, these factors do not always reflect the particular conditions relevant to a firm or industry sector. For example, the carbon intensity of electricity generation may vary widely depending on the energy mix—that is, the share of renewable sources compared with fossil fuels. Using generic emission factors in such cases will result in biased estimates of emissions. Therefore, some organizations may decide to prepare their own customized emission factors, even though such an exercise can be costly and complex.

Overall emission levels vary significantly by region and sector, adding another layer to the complexity of accurate quantification. The emissions related to transport in urban areas are going to be very different from those in rural areas, given differences in infrastructure, fuel types, and travel patterns. Similarly, some heavy industries, such as cement manufacturing and steel production, have very unique emission profiles, which makes it even more difficult to apply the same method of calculating emissions for all sectors. These sectoral and geographical differences highlight the challenges of creating standardized and universal methods for carbon measurement.

In addition to variations in sectoral and geographical measurements, the inconsistency and lack of standardization in emissions reporting, even within the same industry in the same location, pose a major challenge.[4] Different organizations may use different metrics, emission factors, or reporting periods, making comparison of the emissions by companies, sectors, or geographical regions challenging. Although initiatives such as the Carbon Disclosure Project and the TCFD are helping to bring greater consistency and transparency to emissions reporting, differences still persist, and without an international standard, carbon assessment remains inconsistent and often inaccurate.

Measuring carbon emissions is a complex but necessary task in our response to climate change. Many of the available approaches to measuring these emissions entail their own difficulties, ranging from data availability and accuracy issues to the complexity inherent in measuring Scope 3 emissions. However, technology—especially through remote sensing and improved modeling techniques—can improve the accuracy of measurements, especially in measuring large-scale emissions. As corporations and governmental bodies increasingly commit to climate targets, improving carbon accounting will be critical to achieving global climate goals and ensuring accountability in carbon reduction efforts.

QUANTIFICATION OF CLIMATE RISKS FOR ORGANIZATIONS

Climate change is accelerating, and its impacts are now more pronounced. There have been increased calls by organizations worldwide to appropriately understand and quantify climate risks. Organizations are motivated to assess and manage climate-related risks because of regulatory requirements, investor expectations, and the potential physical and financial impacts of climate change on their operations. Climate-related risks can be categorized into physical risk and transition risk. Physical risk refers to the direct impacts of climate change on an organization's assets, operations, and supply chains. Physical risk can be further classified into acute physical risk and chronic physical risk. Acute risk arises from sudden and extreme events such as hurricanes, floods, and wildfires, and chronic risk arises from long-term changes in temperature, precipitation, and sea levels. The impacts of these two types of physical risks could disrupt operations, cause infrastructure damage, and affect supply chains, which create financial losses, productivity impairment, and reputational damage.

Conversely, because governments, investors, and consumers are demanding changes in business practices, organizations might face various risks due to changes in regulations, shifts in market preferences, and technological advances. These risks are called transition risks. Transition risks can arise from more stringent environmental rules and regulations; for example, when carbon pricing or emission caps (e.g., the Carbon Border Adjustment Mechanism by the European Union) are introduced, companies are faced with higher costs. Transition risk can also be caused by changes in consumer behaviors, such as people buying greener products and moving away from carbon-intensive products.

Because both physical and transition risks impact a company's bottom line, the key is for companies to understand and quantify both sets of risks so that they can prepare for future uncertainties and align their business strategies with a rapidly changing climate.

Quantification of climate risks involves applying various methodologies in assessing potential physical and transition-related impacts of climate change on organizations. In the following section, we aim to provide an overview of the available methodologies that can help an organization measure risks caused by climate change.

Scenario Analysis

Scenario analysis is widely applied in the assessment of both physical and transition risks. To conduct a scenario analysis, organizations must first determine the type of climate risk (physical versus transition) they are exposed to and then set goals, such as reducing supply chain vulnerability or improving resilience. Next, organizations have to select relevant climate scenarios. Common scenarios include a pessimistic one with little policy intervention about climate change that leads to high emissions and severe physical risks, usually in a 4°C increase pathway. There will also be a low-emission scenario, which is a more proactive case where increases in global temperature are limited to 1.5°C through sharp emission reductions. This scenario would be more compatible with the Paris Agreement. Lastly, a more plausible, or intermediate, pathway is included, where temperature goes up by 2–3°C with moderate policies. These pathways are usually aligned with the Shared Socioeconomic Pathways (SSPs) developed by the Intergovernmental Panel on Climate Change (IPCC) or Network for Greening the Financial System (NGFS) scenarios or other frameworks that define possible climate outcomes based on different policy and technological scenarios.

Scenario analysis relies on climate models to calculate the physical impacts of sea level rise, increased frequency and/or severity of extreme climate events, and changes in temperature or precipitation levels under different projected conditions. Scenario analysis then identifies which assets and operations are exposed to these risks and the likelihood and severity of the impacts these assets and operations face over time. In quantifying the risks, organizations rely on financial models to estimate the climate impact on asset revaluation, insurance costs, or supply chain disruptions. These can be captured by measures such as revenue loss from extreme weather events, cost increases from carbon taxes, or capital expenditures related to flood defense. Assessing the probabilistic outcome of climate risks, such as the likelihood of flooding inundating warehouses, may require Monte Carlo simulations, a technique that runs a large number of simulations with varying inputs to determine the probability of different climate outcomes.

Based on the scenario analysis, organizations can adjust their business models and develop strategic responses. They might shift to renewable energy, spend additional capital to improve infrastructure resilience, or increase supply chain diversification to reduce their dependence on climate-sensitive regions. Scenario analysis can also reveal climate opportunities. For example, with rising temperatures, colder regions may start to experience higher crop yield. Higher emission standards may also lead to increased adoption of electric vehicles and faster switching to renewables, creating opportunities for companies in those markets.

One of the biggest challenges with conducting an accurate scenario analysis is the inherent uncertainty in climate projections. Climate modeling is based on assumptions about future emission levels, such as long-term trends in technological development, population growth, and public policy. All of these factors are interrelated and constantly evolving. As a result, the selection of credible climate pathways and the outcomes of scenario analysis need to be adjusted constantly. This may prove to be a challenge for some organizations.

Financial Modeling

Climate risks can also be quantified using financial models, which convert identified climate risks into monetary terms. Financial models first identify the key physical and transition risk factors and then calculate their potential impact on the financial outcomes of an organization. For instance, an organization can try to estimate the financial losses resulting from severe weather events such as hurricanes or floods that disrupt its operations. The losses may include direct damages to these physical assets and also lost revenues due to an inability to operate for a period of time because of the climate event disruption. To assess the financial impact, organizations can use historical data from similar events, industry-specific benchmarks, and climate projections to estimate the likelihood and severity of such events on its operations in the future.[5] The estimated financial impacts allow companies to weigh the potential costs of physical climate risks against the potential costs of implementing some mitigation measures, such as infrastructure reinforcement or asset relocation.

Similarly, transition risks can also be monetized through financial modeling. This means estimating the financial impacts arising from changes in regulations, shifts in consumer preferences, or technological advances. For example, an energy company may try to calculate the financial impact of higher carbon prices on its crude oil production. Or a company that specializes in internal combustion engine vehicles may try to estimate the loss in revenue due to consumers switching to electric vehicles. Of course, when conducting financial modeling, one needs to include assumptions about future policy changes, market changes, and prices of renewable energy and low-carbon technologies.

Calculating risk-adjusted returns is an integral part of financial modeling. In general, risks are integrated into investment decisions by adjusting expected returns. For climate risks, companies need to adjust their returns accounting for risks posed by climate change. This means that when calculating discounted cash flows, companies now have to adjust their projections based on climate risks, for example by accounting for higher insurance premiums, possible regulatory penalties, or the costs of adapting to climate change. There can also be revenue shocks due to supply chain disruptions from extreme weather events or a decline in fossil fuel demand. Stranded assets may become a problem as well when there are write-downs of carbon-intensive assets in a net-zero scenario. All of these would imply a higher discount rate when calculating risk-adjusted returns. By incorporating climate-related risks into their valuation or financial models, organizations can make more informed capital allocation decisions and ensure that their portfolios are more resilient to future climate disruptions.

Geospatial Analysis of Climate Data

Climate risks are inherently spatial and are often characterized by strong geographical variability. Therefore, geospatial analysis of climate data is becoming ever more important if we wish to quantify physical risks accurately at a granular level. Climate data includes datasets on past, current, and future climatic conditions, such as temperature, precipitation, wind speed, sea-level rise, and extreme weather events.[6] Geospatial analysis utilizes cartographic technologies, geographic information systems (GIS), and spatial data to model the impacts of climate risks on specific locations, assets, and supply chains.[7]

One type of geospatial analysis uses flood risk modeling. Organizations can use historical flood data combined with projected climate scenarios to identify flood-prone areas near their facilities or those of their suppliers. By overlaying flood risk exposure information on geospatial maps of assets and infrastructure, organizations can identify the areas that are at high risk of being flooded and then estimate the potential financial impacts associated with this exposure. Similarly, organizations can use geospatial analysis to estimate potential risks on their assets from other extreme weather events, such as wildfires, hurricanes, and heatwaves, and simulate how exposure to these types of events might change over time under different climate scenarios.

Geospatial analysis is also performed to understand the physical vulnerability of supply chains. In today's world, even something that is made in the United States can have its inputs and machinery sourced globally. Therefore, a company could use GIS to map the locations of their suppliers and then evaluate each location's risk exposure to climate change–related events. Similar to other models we have outlined so far, geospatial analysis can help organizations understand the financial impact of climate change on their operations in specific locations and develop corresponding risk mitigation strategies, such as diversifying suppliers or relocating some of its operations.

Risk Sensitivity and Stress Testing

A crucial part of quantifying climate-related risks involves sensitivity analysis and stress testing. By changing some assumptions and conditions, organizations can learn how sensitive their operations and investments are to climate-driven changes. In risk sensitivity analysis, organizations first identify the critical driver(s) of climate risks, be it temperature rise or carbon price increase, and then adjust one variable at a time (e.g., increase the carbon tax from thirty to fifty dollars per ton) to determine its isolated effect.

In contrast, stress testing involves testing an organization's resilience under extreme but plausible scenarios, such as a 3°C warming, a category 5 hurricane hitting a production facility, or a $100 per ton carbon tax. A stress test would simulate the potential impacts of these plausible yet catastrophic climate events and then evaluate an organization's ability to withstand them. Stress tests, therefore, focus on multivariable worst-case scenarios, whereas sensitivity analyses focus on single-variable adjustment. Both help organizations identify critical vulnerabilities and determine whether existing climate-related strategies are sufficient to cope with the potential impacts of the most severe climate disruptions.

Integrating Climate Risk Into Enterprise Risk Management

Climate risk is no longer a niche but a mainstream concern of business. Once we are able to quantify the impacts of climate for companies and their supply chains, we need to integrate them into an organization's overall enterprise risk management (ERM) system. This integration is a critical step to developing a coordinated response to climate-related challenges. ERM processes usually involve the identification, assessment, and management of all types of risks an organization could face. Now it must also include risks associated with climate change.

Organizations can use tools such as heat maps to illustrate the relative magnitude and likelihood of different types of climate risks.[8] These climate risks, including physical and transition risks, can then be integrated into the wider risk management frameworks with clear plans for mitigation and adaptation. Informed by the ERM process, organizations can then develop contingency plans to address extreme weather events, such as allocating the necessary resources to build climate-resilient infrastructure or developing strategies to deal with the transition risks arising from carbon regulation and changing market conditions.

Climate is average weather over a thirty-year period. The past ten years have been the hottest ten years on record, and much of the climate change we will experience in the next twenty years will not change even if we stopped consuming all carbon today. It is apparent that extreme weather events are on the rise because of climate change. For organizations to be resilient in the face of these risks, they need to build ERM systems that incorporate climate risk. We have discussed many methods that can help organizations quantify climate risks in this chapter, including scenario analysis, financial modeling, geospatial analysis, and stress testing. All of these methods provide organizations with tools that can offer critical information on how climate change might influence their operations, supply chains, and financial performance. They can also provide information on the opportunities provided by the transition toward a low-carbon economy.

CLIMATE DISCLOSURE FRAMEWORKS

We have discussed sustainability metrics and their disclosure by organizations in previous chapters. Individuals and corporations are increasingly affected by extreme weather events caused at least partly by climate change. The evolution of climate disclosures reflects this growing awareness of climate risks and the demand for greater corporate accountability. The development of climate disclosure can be categorized into distinct phases, demonstrating the increased integration of climate concerns into the management frameworks of corporations and financial institutions globally. This section outlines the many disclosure frameworks for carbon emissions and climate risks.

Carbon Disclosure Project

Climate-related reporting started with voluntary initiatives such as the ones developed by the Carbon Disclosure Project (CDP). Founded in 2000, CDP was among the earliest global initiatives focused on promoting corporate accountability with regard to climate-related dangers and emissions of greenhouse gases (GHGs). CDP developed one of the earliest standardized frameworks for companies to report their climate impact and mitigation strategies, playing a pioneering role in the development of early climate disclosure practices.

CDP's initial work involved obtaining data through detailed questionnaires distributed to companies. The first questionnaire was sent in 2003 to the largest publicly traded companies in the world. This questionnaire contained detailed questions on GHG emissions, climate-related risks, and mitigation strategies of companies. Some of the questions asked for absolute and intensity-based GHG emission levels, governance mechanisms for climate oversight, and certain climate-related risks and opportunities.[9] Among the main questions included in the early CDP surveys were questions on Scope 1 and Scope 2 emissions. Later iterations included Scope 3 emissions, standardized by the Greenhouse Gas Protocol (GHGP) in 2011 to promote transparency along the entire value chain. The categorization of emissions into three "scopes" was developed by the World Resource Institute (WRI) and the World Business Council for Sustainable Development (WBCSD) in their GHGP. It is now the foundational tool for organizations to report their emissions and align with climate reporting initiatives such as the CDP or TCFD. There are other standards such as the ISO 14064, which follows GHGP, but further breaks down Scope 1 into stationary combustion, mobile combustion, and fugitive emissions and Scope 3 into upstream and downstream emissions, offering a more granular approach.

Energy use and efficiency were also among the major focus areas. Companies were asked for information on their total energy consumption levels and to describe the measures they implemented to improve energy efficiency and the efforts they undertook to switch to renewable energy sources. In addition, the CDP framework encouraged companies to report their targets for emissions reduction, expressed either in absolute reduction goals, such as reducing emissions by a certain percentage by a specific year, or as intensity-based reduction targets tied to production or revenue.

The CDP questionnaire also included questions about the risks and opportunities resulting from climate change. Companies were required to answer questions about their specific exposure to physical and transition risks. At the same time, CDP encouraged companies to identify and report potential opportunities arising from low-carbon transitions, such as investments made in low-carbon technologies or renewable energy projects.

Another significant component of the early CDP framework had to do with governance and accountability. Respondents were asked to describe the processes through which climate-related risks were managed at their organizations, including whether climate policies and resiliency were under the jurisdiction of the board of directors or dedicated committees. Over time, the CDP questionnaire went beyond carbon and expanded its scope to include disclosure questions on water usage, water-risk exposure, and impacts from forest ecosystems.

The CDP differed from other disclosure regimes due to its scoring system. Organizations are given scores for the completeness and quality of their responses to the CDP annual questionnaire. The scores then lead to ratings from A (Leadership) to D (Disclosure). In 2023, out of the 21,000 companies being scored by CDP, 361 made the climate change A list.[10] These scores provide stakeholders with a straightforward method to assess how well companies are handling and reporting their climate-related risks. The clarity of the scoring framework allows investors and other stakeholders to identify leaders in sustainability. For companies, a high CDP score can boost an organization's reputation, help attract investment, and provide evidence of their commitment to climate action, whereas a low score can trigger an internal review and call for improvement.

A number of leading companies responded to CDP's initial disclosure requests. Energy companies like BP and Shell released emissions data along with their investments in cleaner energy technologies, setting up the benchmark for accountability in high-emission industries.[11] The early work of CDP provided a base for subsequent frameworks such as the TCFD, which adopted many of the principles established by CDP. Even today, CDP continues to play a substantial role in the evolution of climate disclosures, setting ambitious benchmarks for corporate environmental accountability and expanding its scope to address emerging sustainability challenges. In 2023, over 23,000 companies from various industries worldwide disclosed their climate impact through CDP, representing two-thirds of global market capitalization.[12]

Successes notwithstanding, CDP has a number of challenges. One major challenge relates to the heterogeneity in climate-related disclosures across different regions and sectors. Although the standardized questionnaire designed by CDP helps to some extent to overcome this challenge, the quality and specificity of the responses still vary considerably. Some companies provide very detailed reports that follow international standards, such as those of the TCFD, whereas others report very limited or unclear information. Moreover, the lack of independent verification of the data submitted by entities may lead to questions about the credibility of the information presented. As demand for transparency grows, organizations such as the CDP and other sustainability reporting platforms will have to face these challenges to ensure their disclosures meet the evolving needs of investors, regulators, and other relevant stakeholders. In our view, as stated previously, only government-mandated disclosure with the possibility of sanctions for inaccurate disclosure can assure accurate measurement and reporting.

Task Force on Climate-Related Financial Disclosures

The next phase in climate disclosure saw a move toward more standardized frameworks for climate-related disclosures. In the 2010s, initiatives such as the Global Reporting Initiative and the Sustainability Accounting Standards Board provided structured and sectoral guidelines for organizations to disclose environmental and sustainability metrics. We have covered these guidelines extensively in chapter 3 of this book. A key milestone was the formation of the Task Force on Climate-Related Financial Disclosures (TCFD). In 2015, the Financial Stability Board (FSB) was established to formulate a framework for the disclosure of climate-related financial risks. This framework aimed to inform corporate decision-makers about the influence of climate change on the financial stability of companies through the adoption of standardized metrics that can track and report on the associated risks and opportunities of climate change. The framework was mainly designed to assist investors, lenders, and various stakeholders in making informed decisions concerning the climate-related impacts on corporations and financial institutions.

Before TCFD, climate disclosure was rare for companies, and climate-related reporting was often fragmented and inconsistent, with no standard for the type and quality of information companies should provide.[13] Most companies either did not report or disclosed only limited, qualitative, or broad statements concerning financial risks related to climate change. The quality and quantity of reporting made it very difficult for investors to understand what was at stake financially from climate-related risks. As the impacts of climate change became more severe by the day, both in the United States and globally, it became clear that climate risks—ranging from transition risks involving regulatory changes and market shifts to physical risks stemming from extreme weather events—needed to be taken seriously by the financial sector. The TCFD improved the standardization of the disclosure metrics, many of which are quantitative indicators that allow for the evaluation of financial impacts of climate risks and opportunities.

The TCFD's recommended frameworks are structured around four key pillars: governance, strategy, risk management, and metrics/targets.[14] The first of these pillars, governance, focuses on requiring organizations to disclose how their boards and senior management oversee and address climate-related risks and opportunities. This pillar encourages companies to describe how climate risks are being integrated into the corporate governance structure, including listing the specific role the board plays in overseeing climate-related issues and how top-level management incorporates climate considerations and initiatives into corporate strategy and daily operations.

The strategy pillar requires organizations to disclose how climate change affects their business models, financial planning processes, and strategic objectives. Companies are encouraged to assess both physical and transition risks and the short- and long-term implications of these risks for their business models and operations. The strategy pillar also calls on companies to include climate-related considerations into their financial planning processes, including, for example, updating their revenue forecast to account for shifts in consumer behavior toward sustainable products or green services, adjusting capital expenditure—such as investment in low-carbon technology or energy efficiency—to be more resilient, and reviewing cost structures that may be impacted significantly as a result of climate-related regulations or resource depletion. Given the uncertainties associated with future climate predictions and their associated impacts, the TCFD encourages organizations to utilize scenario analysis to test the resilience of their financial plans under various climate-related scenarios (i.e., with different levels of climate warming).

The third pillar, risk management, is about the process for identifying, assessing, and addressing climate-related risks within an organization's broader risk management framework. The TCFD recommends that organizations and companies disclose their processes for integrating climate risk into their overall enterprise risk management framework and encourages organizations to take into consideration how climate-related risks are identified across business units and how these risks are assessed for materiality and significance to the organization's core business. The risk assessment process should evaluate the likelihood of a particular climate-related risk materializing and its time horizon. Of course, once a risk is identified and assessed, an organization needs to manage it through relevant and effective mitigation and adaptation strategies.

The last pillar of the TCFD is about metrics and targets. This pillar focuses on the disclosure of quantitative measures. The TCFD encourages companies to disclose the indicators they are using to assess climate-related risks, manage the risks, and track their progress toward achieving climate-related targets. The metrics often include direct and indirect GHG emissions, carbon intensity of products and services, energy intensity, share of renewable energy, water use indicators, and many others. Moreover, the metrics and targets pillar encourages companies to set climate-related targets. Companies following TCFD often use the Science-Based Targets Initiative (SBTI) to set these targets and ensure the targets meet rigorous climate science criteria. Companies can set five- to ten-year goals as well as long-term targets such as reaching net-zero emission by 2050. The SBTi targets align with limiting global warming to 1.5°C, as required by the Paris Agreement.

Through the four pillars, the TCFD allows companies to integrate climate risk into the core of their financial decision-making processes and facilitates the transition toward increased transparency and standardization of climate disclosures. Since its launch, many jurisdictions, such as the United Kingdom, New Zealand, and the European Union (EU), have integrated TCFD principles into their mandatory reporting requirements, first for large companies and financial institutions. The adoption by major organizations demonstrated a growing recognition that climate-related risks increasingly pose material problems that will affect company bottom lines. The growing number of TCFD-aligned nonfinancial reports and disclosures has also made it easier for investors to evaluate the climate-related risks and opportunities associated with their portfolio companies. Additionally, the TCFD framework influences the development of broader sustainability reporting standards, such as the one being formulated by the International Sustainability Standards Board (ISSB), which closely parallels the methodology advocated by TCFD.[15]

Despite its significant influence, the TCFD faces several challenges. Conducting scenario analysis as recommended by the TCFD is highly complicated, as we previously discussed: companies are encouraged to assess the potential financial impacts of climate-related risks under different climate scenarios, such as those that are consistent with a 2°C or 1.5°C rise in global temperature. However, the local impacts on a company site or supply chain location are very hard to determine, and regional climate models and predictions face huge uncertainties with unreliable estimates of the number and severity of localized climate events. In applying the TCFD framework, organizations often lack specialized knowledge, modeling tools, and data to perform the type of rigorous climate and financial analysis required to understand and then internalize climate-related risks, especially when it comes to small- and medium-sized enterprises (SMEs) or companies located in developing countries. Moreover, the adoption of various TCFD recommendations is still fragmented and inconsistent across regions and sectors, which impedes comparability and hinders the evaluation of the disclosed information across companies.

European Sustainability Reporting Standards Under the Corporate Sustainability Reporting Directive

By the 2020s, climate disclosures became more integrated into financial regulations, reflecting their critical role in corporate risk management. Governments and regulatory bodies around the world began introducing mandatory disclosure requirements. In Europe, climate discourse requirements for corporate sustainability reporting follow the European Sustainability Reporting Standards outlined in the Corporate Sustainability Reporting Directive (CSRD). The CSRD is aligned with the TCFD in reporting physical and transition climate risks and incorporates many aspects of the TCFD recommendations. Under CSRD, companies should comply with the TCFD-aligned approach of reporting on climate risks.

Similar to the TCFD, the CSRD requires companies to report in detail their climate-related activities and risks. This includes (1) climate-related risks and opportunities, (2) governance and oversight of climate risks, and (3) climate strategy and targets.[16] In addition to risk disclosure, entities are expected to report on the opportunities arising as a result of the transition to a low-carbon economy, such as new market opportunities from sustainable products, services, or technologies, as well as potential cost savings from enhanced energy efficiency or improved practices in sustainability.

Governance and oversight risks include board oversight, requiring companies to describe how their corporate governance structures monitor and manage climate-related risks and opportunities. This includes a description of the role of the board and senior management on issues related to climate, strategic decision-making impacting implementation of climate goals, and the integration of climate considerations within the overall business strategy. In addition, companies are required to disclose how climate-related risks (both physical and transition risks) are incorporated into the organization's broader risk management processes. This involves detailing how climate risks are identified, assessed, and managed as part of the company's regular risk management framework.

According to the CSRD, organizations must clearly set out their plans for reducing their GHG emissions. Organizations are required to detail how they will reduce Scope 1, 2, and 3 emissions as well as carbon intensity (emission per dollar of revenue). The complexity of gathering data all along the value chain makes Scope 3 emissions reporting even more complex, although organizations are required either to report on these or to explain why they have been unable to quantify them. More generally, organizations need to perform scenario analyses assessing the potential impacts of climate change on their strategic and operational planning under different hypothetical future climate scenarios—most obviously, temperature-rise scenarios of 1.5°C or 2°C. In the master of science program in sustainability management at Columbia University, we have recently designed a new course on climate risk and scenario analysis to teach our students exactly how to conduct these analyses.

Companies also have to provide a detailed account of the concrete actions they are taking to meet whatever climate targets they set internally. This may include investments in renewable energy, energy efficiency, and decarbonization technologies, such as carbon capture or green hydrogen. Along with the description of such efforts, companies are required to submit reports on the progress made toward the targets. The targets have to align with the goals of the Paris Agreement: limiting global warming to well below 2°C with a best outcome of 1.5°C. Organizations must also disclose any revision they make to their climate goals or actions in light of new developments in climate science or changes in business circumstances. This can include a change of goals or a shift in strategy driven by newly adopted regulations, emerging technologies, or unforeseen risks and opportunities related to climate change. The CSRD thus provides incentives for companies not only to set ambitious climate targets but also to disclose the actions they are taking and the changes they are making to their plans in order to stay aligned with global climate goals.

Last but not least, the CSRD requires independent assurance of sustainability disclosures to make the data reported credible and reliable. The CSRD also expands the scope of companies required to disclose, including SMEs and non-EU companies that operate in the EU market.[17] As the urgency of climate action grows, so too does the need for robust, transparent, and standardized disclosure. The outlined frameworks in this section aim to help organizations measure, manage, and report their climate-related risks and emissions. It also provides companies with the necessary tools to assess financial and operational impacts stemming from climate change and provides investors and stakeholders with the ability to make informed decisions based on consistent and comparable data.

US Securities and Exchange Commission Climate Rule and California Climate Laws

As we discussed in chapter 4, in 2022, the US Securities and Exchange Commission (SEC) issued a landmark set of rules to increase the transparency of corporate disclosures on climate-related risks and their consequent financial impacts. For the first time, publicly traded US companies would be required to disclose in great detail their carbon emissions, the risk associated with climate, and any strategies aimed at addressing climate change. The SEC's carbon disclosure requirements would have made it mandatory for companies listed on the US stock markets to disclose exposures to climate-related risks and the resultant impact on financial performance, aiming at global alignment along the lines of the TCFD. This was a significant development because the US stock market is by far the largest in the world and is where many of the largest companies in the world trade their stocks.

Under the SEC requirements, the reporting of Scope 1 and Scope 2 GHG emissions would have been mandatory; companies would have had to disclose direct and indirect emissions from operations owned or controlled and energy consumed by the company. Disclosure for Scope 3—essentially all indirect emissions arising from the company's value chain—was only required if these emissions were deemed "material" to the company or if the company had set a climate-related target inclusive of such emissions. Companies would have had to assess and disclose the financial impact of climate-related risks, including both physical and transition risks, and explain how their processes for governance and risk management incorporate climatic issues. Firms also would have had to disclose climate targets and progress made toward them, though the proposed rules did not require those targets to be aligned with global climate agreements.

In essence, the SEC's carbon disclosure rules would have provided investors with more reliable, comparable, and consistent information about the potential financial consequences of climate-related risks. This was a significant improvement over the patchwork array of previous voluntary reporting standards, which too often provided inconsistent disclosures that frequently omitted critical information. By requiring all US-listed companies to assess and disclose their GHG emissions, climate risks, and strategies for mitigation, the SEC aimed to align corporate reporting with the growing recognition that climate change poses a material financial risk to many industries.

However, compared to more comprehensive international frameworks, such as the EU's CSRD or California's Senate Bill 253, the SEC's once-proposed rules offered a relatively flexible and less stringent approach, particularly in terms of Scope 3 emissions and third-party verification.[18] Although the rules hoped to mandate climate risk governance and require companies to provide data on emissions and financial impacts, they fell short in mandating comprehensive Scope 3 disclosures or internationally aligned targets and relied on voluntary third-party assurance for certain data, raising concerns about consistency and reliability. Because these rules have now been withdrawn by the second Trump administration, they can only be viewed as an aspirational framework that may someday reemerge.

As we discussed earlier, although the US federal government has withdrawn its carbon reporting requirements, the state of California continues to maintain its own rules. California, the largest US state economy, has developed some of the most stringent carbon disclosure requirements in the country, especially with the introduction of Senate Bills 253 and 261 in 2023. These bills, which require companies doing business in California with annual revenues over $1 billion to disclose their Scope 1, 2, and 3 emissions, go far beyond the SEC's once-proposed rules in several key aspects. First, California's legislation requires companies to report Scope 3 emissions in all cases without the subjective "materiality" test applied by the SEC. This implies that companies will be held accountable for emissions across their entire value chain, eliminating loopholes or self-determination about what is material to report. In addition, California's regulations include specific deadlines for achieving specific emissions reduction targets and align the climate strategies of companies with the state's climate targets. The legislation also mandates third-party verification of reported data, improving accuracy and credibility.

Similarly, the CSRD, which came into effect in 2024, also mandates mandatory disclosures on all three scope emissions, with no exceptions for materiality on Scope 3 emissions.[19] The CSRD also leaves companies with little room to sidestep the reporting of their full carbon footprint. The CSRD requires companies to adopt a double materiality perspective, which means companies have to disclose not only how climate risks affect their financial performance (financial materiality) but also the environmental and social impacts their operations have on the climate (environmental materiality). This double materiality requirement significantly broadens the scope of disclosures. In addition, the EU has set ambitious climate targets in general, pushing companies to achieve targets that are in line with global climate goals. Third-party verification is also mandatory for most types of disclosures under the CSRD, ensuring greater credibility of the reported data.

One of the reasons that governments or government agencies around the world have been working on environmental disclosure rules and metrics is that the vacuum in sustainability metrics and reporting is being filled by a variety of nongovernmental organizations (NGOs) that have designed sustainability metrics and reports and then charge corporations for judging their sustainability.

Global Harmonization with the International Sustainability Standards Board

Because of the fragmentation of diverse sustainability frameworks, there has been a sustained effort to converge to a global standard. This was evidenced first by a joint statement from the major framework providers including the Global Reporting Initiative (GRI), International Integrated Reporting Council (IIRC), Sustainability Accounting Standards Board (SASB), CDP, and Climate Disclosure Standards Board (CDSB), acknowledging a shared vision and their intent to work together toward alignment and comprehensive corporate sustainability reporting.[20] This was later followed by a jointly developed guide by SASB and GRI on how to use both of their standards together for sustainability reporting. Later, the SASB and IIRC, which developed the Integrated Reporting guidelines, consolidated into the Value Reporting Foundation, a merger that significantly simplified the corporate sustainability reporting landscape.

Perhaps the most significant development was the decision by the IFRS Foundation to establish the International Sustainability Standards Board (ISSB) with the mandate to address the fragmented reporting landscape by developing a unified global baseline for sustainability disclosure. To achieve this goal, IFRS merged with the Value Reporting Foundation, which includes SASB and IIRC's Integrated Reporting framework. In leveraging existing frameworks and reducing redundancies in developing its Sustainability

Disclosure Standards, IFRS also integrated content and expertise of the CDSB and the TCFD structure of four key pillars (governance, strategy, risk management, and metrics and targets).

The effort to create a single global system of sustainability metrics and reporting, although laudable, has yet to acknowledge the critical importance of national sovereignty in establishing a reporting system with sanctions for deceptive or incomplete information. The problem with some of the NGO-developed sustainability and climate measures is that, unlike generally accepted financial accounting principles, they are not defined and enforced by a government agency with the ability to impose sanctions. For example, security regulators, such as the SEC in the United States, define financial terms and regulate corporate financial reporting and the firms that audit publicly traded corporations. Publicly traded companies pay attention to the SEC because the commission controls and influences access to capital markets. In contrast, the NGOs generate revenues from corporations and idealistic donors and have no way of ensuring that corporate sustainability reports are based in fact.

CONCLUSION

The measurement and disclosure of carbon emissions and climate risks are critical pieces to the evolving landscape of corporate sustainability. As organizations face increasing pressure from governments, investors, and other stakeholders to address the environmental and social consequences of their operations, the accurate quantification and transparent reporting of climate-related risks have become more important. We also expect that this requirement will soon expand to include biodiversity, ecological damage, the impact of toxics, and other types of air, water, and land pollution.

The frameworks and methodologies discussed in this chapter, such as scenario analysis, financial modeling, geospatial analysis, and stress testing, provide useful tools for organizations to assess the physical and transition risks posed by climate change. These methods, summarized in figure 6.1, enable companies to better

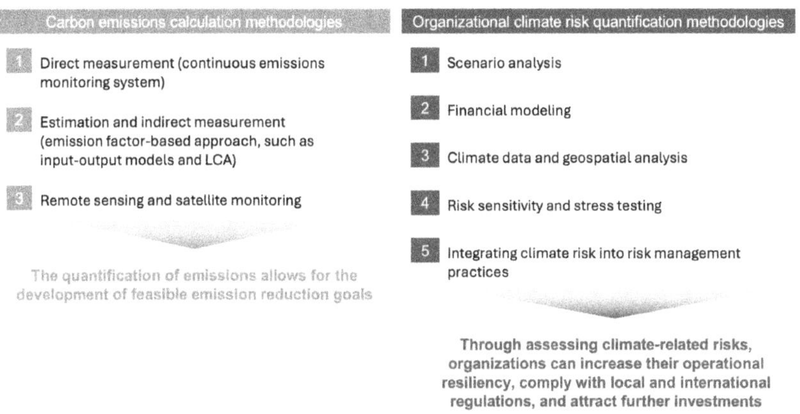

Figure 6.1 Summary of the Major Practices and Methodologies of Climate Risk Assessment and Reporting

understand the potential financial impacts and opportunities arising from climate change and then incorporate this knowledge into their long-term strategic planning.

As climate risks, such as extreme weather events and policy-driven transitions, become central to financial performance, climate disclosures are increasingly viewed as essential information for investors and diverse stakeholders. As we have outlined in this chapter, climate disclosures have evolved from voluntary, fragmented practices to mandatory and standardized requirements that are integral to corporate governance and financial systems. Many companies, especially the larger ones, have already begun to align their climate reporting with financial disclosures. With growing regulatory requirements and a global effort to harmonize standards (e.g., both the SEC climate rules and the European Sustainability Reporting Standards under CSRD would have aligned with TCFD's core principles), climate disclosures have become a critical tool in managing climate change risks for organizations and for more broadly aligning with global objectives such as the Paris Agreement and the Sustainable Development Goals.

Despite the issues we have discussed in consolidating fragmented frameworks, the need for generally accepted sustainability metrics remains, and the journey toward comprehensive and standardized climate risk measurement and disclosure is not without other challenges. Data availability and accuracy remain significant hurdles, particularly for Scope 3 emissions, which require collaboration across supply chains and the development of reliable emission factors. Moreover, the lack of global consistency in reporting standards and methodologies complicates efforts to compare performance across sectors and geographies. To address the challenge of fragmented standards, initiatives like the ISSB were launched in 2021 to unify existing frameworks, including those from the TCFD and the SASB, into a global standard.

Looking ahead, the continued development of technology, artificial intelligence, and data analytics will enhance the accuracy and timeliness of carbon emissions measurement, and advancements in climate models and satellite monitoring can provide even more detailed insights into climate impacts. In sum, the integration of carbon and climate risk measurement and disclosure into sustainability management frameworks is essential for building a resilient future. Companies that adopt these practices are not only future-proofing their operations against climate-related disruptions but also contributing to the broader effort to mitigate global climate change.

7

CONCLUSION

Environmental Risk, Financial Risk, and Effective Management in a Complex, Technological, and Global Economy

There is a close relationship among environmental risk, financial risk, and management effectiveness in today's complex, technology-driven global economy. Environmental and financial risk, the recruitment and retention of talent, and positive engagement with stakeholders and customers are central elements of successful organizational strategy and management. We live in a more observed and communication-obsessed world. Organizational actions are examined constantly, and very little—even what organizations consider proprietary—is truly private. Disinformation is ubiquitous, and it is sometimes difficult to separate fact from myth. Nevertheless, organizations can no longer isolate themselves from their environment. They need to understand the physical, social, cultural, political, and financial dimensions of their operations, stakeholders, and markets.

UNDERSTANDING AND MANAGING TECHNOLOGICAL COMPLEXITY

The overall theme of this work is the need for more mindful and careful management. This is not an argument against innovation, entrepreneurship, risk-taking, and creativity. But in order to take risks, it is critical that we understand the environment in which we are operating. Risks should be calculated, not charged into. Management must understand the market in which they compete, the talent required for production, the physical constraints and opportunities surrounding them, the capital requirements for maintenance and expansion, and the technological requirements for production: the list is long, and this is only a sample of the knowledge needed for effective management. One of the reasons that decision-making requires more analytics and quantitative data is that as we collect more data, we require more information to understand what we are doing and the world within which we are doing it.

Management requires more sophistication because the world has become more crowded and complicated. The nature of work has been transformed by technology, but to a considerable extent, the politicians running our governments haven't fully figured this out yet. The hardware in your iPhone is worth much less than the software and applications that run on it. The high value-added part of our economy is in creativity, design, communications, strategy, and analysis. Manufacturing is necessary, but it is not as profitable as services, including the *design* of production processes. Humans are social creatures, and the technologies of communication, information, and transportation send many of us all over the world in search of opportunity, travel, and productive advantage.

Understanding and managing technology within an organization requires scientific literacy. Although Silicon Valley and other managers in the tech business often have technical and scientific backgrounds, most managers come from law, finance, marketing, public policy, and management, and few have technical backgrounds. This leads to managers who are ignorant of climate science, medical science, computer science, and other forms of expertise central to our economy. Science is simply denied when it results in "inconvenient truths," and some of these folks consider it less important than image, spin, and the ability to dominate and beat one's enemies. It doesn't matter if cigarettes, fossil fuels, toxic waste, and addictive drugs harm people and the planet as long as there is money to be made. Being noticed and appearing to be in charge enable one to somehow "control" reality. This willful ignorance and retreat to propaganda are a deep threat to our long-term well-being. It is also the wrong strategy. We can make some money by ignoring the costs of technology as long as there are benefits. But we can make more money and produce more long-term well-being by ensuring that the new technologies we develop and use have the least negative impact possible while producing the most possible benefit. *We are arguing for a strategy of being smart instead of stupid.*

We are also arguing for thoughtfulness. The scientists who developed the atomic bomb and nearly all of the people who decided to use it thought long and hard about the technology they had built and used. Some were shocked by the bomb's destructive power, and at the time, few understood the long-term impact of a radioactive explosion. They thought deeply about what was lost and gained. Today, we see the impact that texting and driving has, and we move to regulate it, but we are only slowly starting to think about the impact of endless information, images, and communication on our minds, cultures, families, and relationships. Our casual, blasé ignorance about technology is only matched by its massive impact on our daily existence.

We have reason to be concerned about the impact of technological complexity on our lives and on our representative democracy. The growth of unelected experts in governmental decision-making makes it difficult for elected representatives to influence complex decisions. Linkage from the public to their representatives and then to technical experts rarely takes place and only happens when issues are urgent. The process of communicating the impact of new technologies or newly understood problems is far from perfect. Additionally, technological complexity is matched by economic complexity and the sheer number of decisions that must be made each day to keep our society and economy functioning. In place of the difficult process of communicating and simplifying and understanding complexity, we see the growth of conspiracy theories, disinformation, and pure falsehoods endlessly communicated on social media.

A key issue of sustainability management is to ensure that those who participate in decision-making have at least a basic understanding of the science and technology they are managing. In many organizations, we are seeing the development of professional staffers whose job includes translating science to nonscientists and communicating management issues, political feasibility, and market realities to technical experts. In the past half-century, the technical complexity of our world has increased exponentially: low-cost computing, mobile and inexpensive communication, GPS, the web, streaming music and video, countless drugs and advances in medical technology, improved energy storage and renewable energy technology, drones and driverless vehicles—the list of new technologies is virtually endless. What has remained the same is human biology and brainpower. Our ability to absorb information does not grow very much, so the nature of information itself must constantly evolve. Everything is summarized, and we have less and less understanding of the details of actions and technology that affect our lives. We need to hire a consultant or call a help desk to turn on our television. Yes, we have unlimited entertainment whenever we want it, but how many of us have the slightest idea of how it works? This is one area where we see the potential benefits and harms of artificial intelligence. Artificial intelligence can help us manage complexity but could also increase our ignorance of how the world and our technology actually work. The danger of artificial intelligence is simply a subset of the danger of technologies that are not controlled and understood by the humans leading our organizations and society.

There is no way for any one person to understand all of the science that we come into contact with, and we need to have an informed discussion of the definition of scientific literacy in our increasingly technological world. How much must we know to be informed citizens, organizational staff, and managers? Our view on this is that there is a baseline of understanding of physics, chemistry, ecology, and biology that everyone needs, but then the specifics will depend on the organization being managed. What is critical is the ability to learn constantly and be open to new knowledge and ideas. The notion that once you graduate from formal education you can stop learning is completely ridiculous.

The management of technical complexity requires sustainability metrics and key performance indicators that are built on a foundation of scientific understanding and fact. When defining success, we need to understand its causes and, similarly, the causes of failure. Some of these causal variables are technical. If a key performance indicator involves reducing the costs of waste disposal, we need to understand the economics of waste transport and landfill tipping fees, but we also need to understand the environmental impact of landfill emissions and effluent discharges. When we develop summary measures, we necessarily reduce our attention to detail, so we must ensure these measures truly summarize the key factors we are trying to understand and manage.

Although technology can cause environmental damage, it can also typically reduce damage as well. Catalytic converters and power plant stack scrubbers reduced air pollution dramatically. Electric vehicles and renewable energy further reduce air pollution but simultaneously create other environmental problems, such as toxics and fires from batteries and environmental damage from mining. The technology of artificial intelligence and robotics will enable us to mine our waste stream for resources, reducing the need to mine materials from the planet. But those same technologies will be difficult to control without effective regulation and human governance.

THE IMPORTANCE AND RISKS OF GLOBAL SUPPLY CHAINS

Advances in communication, transportation, and information have facilitated the development of goods and services built on intricate, global supply chains as well as what we have termed supply webs: interconnected supply chains that are built to permit greater redundancy. We discovered our extreme dependence on supply chains during the COVID-19 pandemic when some were interrupted due to plant and port shutdowns. On the service side of the equation, technologies like Zoom permitted the continuation and deepening of global networks. On the manufacturing side, we saw production problems as shipping was disrupted, leading to scarcity and inflation. Inflation was exacerbated by governments flooding the economy with payments to families and businesses to enable survival during an economic crisis. In 2025, we learned that real and threatened tariffs started and stopped by an unpredictable US president could also disrupt global supply chains. All of this brought home the degree to which political and environmental shocks can impact the risks encountered by businesses.

Understanding and projecting risk in an uncertain, interconnected, and complex world have become more important. Politicians seeking to reduce this risk retreat to nationalistic solutions such as tariffs and other devices to reduce interdependency. In our view, that is a self-defeating strategy. Technology, information, transportation, and communication are responsible for facilitating the construction of highly efficient and highly specialized supply chains and webs. This enables companies to produce high-quality goods and services at the lowest possible cost. Companies will do everything they need to do to continue to construct supply chains and webs regardless of the actions of government. Without them, they are vulnerable to price and quality competition from organizations that are able to construct higher-quality and lower-priced supplies, products, or services.

The global economy and global corporations are a fact of economic life that must be understood and managed. Globalization brings greater risks to organizations along with greater potential benefits. This is what sustainability metrics and management are designed to cope with. Efforts to end globalization will fail. Globalization can only be understood and managed; it is driven by irresistible market forces. Public policy must be developed to reduce globalization's impact on workers. Globalization results in less predictable and stable labor markets that require a greater emphasis on worker training and education to provide marketable skills in a rapidly changing economic environment. The failure of government to pay attention to the impact of technology and workers inevitably leads to political instability. It also leads to labor scarcity that can be addressed through enhanced training and education.

Global supply chains help organizations produce higher-quality and lower-priced goods and services but can lead to environmental damage from the energy used in shipping and the materials needed for packaging. More energy-efficient shipping might someday rely on wind power, biofuels, and solar power on transport ships. Packaging material might be recycled on these ships and again used in packaging, adding an element of circularity to supply chain production.

Authoritarian and nationalistic forces used COVID-19 as an opportunity to restrict people and businesses to stay within their borders,[1] but in the long run, the forces of technology, economic development, and human curiosity will not be contained. When the COVID lockdowns ended, global trade rapidly accelerated. Globalization has its downside, making governance in the public interest more difficult and complex, but instead of trying to shut it down, we need to figure out how to make it work. We are living on a planet that will remain governed by sovereign nations, but we need to get better at regulating global commerce. Individuals, families, communities, and nations pursue self-interest. That is a given. We seek advantage and try to get ahead. But competition does not make cooperation impossible, and global rules of the game can facilitate rather than impede competition. Xenophobia and racism are obstacles to achieving sustainable economic development. Understanding the history and motivation of people from other places can help us learn more about each other and makes cooperation easier and more effective. And the internet can be a tool for sharing images and information globally. We know it is capable of magnifying disinformation and misunderstanding, but its capacity for truth-telling can't be understated. Shared visual images cannot be refuted and are seen throughout the world. The planet we live on has been made smaller and more accessible by the World Wide Web. Economic development, like communication, is also global.

Global supply chains are a fact of economic life. They are built on geographic, historic, and cultural distinctions between people and places. Different places and people come to specialize in producing different things. We are able to bring those specialties together in a supply chain. These chains rely on inexpensive communication, information, and transportation and enable higher-quality and lower-priced goods and services. The economic and technological forces behind these trends are irresistible. Nationalist political leaders will lose the battle to influence global corporations if their political strategy does not include an understanding of the economic benefits of globalization.

Some politicians in the United States are eager to rebuild American manufacturing. Nostalgia for labor-intensive, blue-collar industries is impairing their judgment. Although the political appeal of this nostalgia is obvious, it is a vision built on a fantasy. Rebuilding American manufacturing is a good idea that will diversify our economy, but let's face it, the factories of the future will be largely automated and run from control rooms rather than factory floors. They will not result in mass employment. If you visit a modern auto plant, you will see hundreds, not thousands, of workers. If you go to a skyscraper construction site, where once thousands of workers connected steel girders and cemented bricks in place, today you see far fewer workers connecting modular walls and floors manufactured in a highly automated factory and assembled at the building site. We are in a brain-based, service-oriented economy. Millions of people are unemployed and underemployed, and effective and practical vocational training is required to remedy that deep problem. Manual labor and manufacturing will be with us for a long time, but automation and artificial intelligence are changing the nature of work, and effective organizations are learning how to utilize these amazing, if sometimes scary, tools.

Globalization must be tamed rather than eliminated. The advantages of immigration should be obvious in a brain-based economy. If one runs an organization and can recruit staff from a planet of over eight billion people instead of a nation of 330 million, the odds are they will recruit a more talented staff. That means the organization will be more creative and innovative, and a globally staffed organization will tend to win in a free, competitive marketplace. The nation, city, or organization that is most welcoming to people from all over the world and offers the highest quality of life has an edge in the global competition for talent. Regulating and reducing the immigration of talented staff to preserve jobs for less talented local people is a losing strategy.

One of the reasons New York City and other global cities came back after the COVID-19 pandemic is their attractiveness to talented people. In New York City, 40 percent of residents were born in other nations. Cohen and Eimicke were born here, as were their parents, but if you go back another generation, both are descended from immigrants. Guo was born in China and is a first-generation New Yorker. New York City's immigrant population doesn't count Eimicke and Cohen, and it doesn't include foreign students, tourists, and people in the city illegally. Young, ambitious, and talented people (like Guo Dong) are attracted to the city's energy, dynamism, opportunity, and excitement. Diversity is not simply valuable for reasons of ethics and ideology; it facilitates the creation of groups better able to deal with complexity. Modern production systems are complicated and have many fixed and moving parts. Think of all the skills and talent required to create a movie. You need experts in storytelling, lighting, filming, sound recording, sound mixing, editing, set construction, acting, directing, costume design, makeup, and scores of other skills. When we work to address a problem in the field of environmental sustainability, we often need lawyers, policy analysts, engineers, health scientists, ecologists, environmental scientists, management specialists, communication specialists, and a wide variety of other experts. The life experiences that help build expertise vary. We need people from many places and with many backgrounds, and they need to be good at working in heterogeneous groups. Experience working in a team with members from many places and with varied histories is a particularly sought-after twenty-first-century professional skill.

The communities that are built for homogeneity will lose to those built for diversity. Communities that welcome people with different backgrounds will be better able to attract the talent needed to compete. This is not an argument for open borders and immigration at will. Quite the contrary, it is an argument for encouraging the immigration of talented people and their families and building on a central American heritage. With few exceptions, we are a nation of immigrants. Some of us were brought here unwillingly, and others came illegally, but we are fundamentally the planet's most global nation. We should build on and take great pride in that diversity and recognize the advantage it provides us in the competition to attract talent from every corner of the world. This was a point made by John F. Kennedy in his book *A Nation of Immigrants*[2] and by Ronald Reagan at the end of his second term as president on January 19, 1989, when he observed:

> Since this is the last speech that I will give as President, I think it's fitting to leave one final thought, an observation about a country which I love. It was stated best in a letter I received not long ago. A man wrote me and said: "You can go to live in France, but you cannot become a Frenchman. You can go to live in Germany or Turkey or Japan, but you cannot become a German, a Turk, or Japanese. But anyone, from any corner of the Earth, can come to live in America and become an American." . . . This, I believe, is one of the most important sources of America's greatness. We lead the world because, unique among nations, we draw our people—our strength—from every country and every corner of the world. And by doing so we continuously renew and enrich our nation. While other countries cling to the stale past, here in America we breathe life into dreams. We create the future, and the world follows us into tomorrow. Thanks to each wave of new arrivals to this land of opportunity, we're a nation forever young, forever bursting with energy and new ideas, and always on the cutting edge, always leading the world to the next frontier. This quality is vital to our future as a nation. If we ever closed the door to new Americans, our leadership in the world would soon be lost.[3]

The United States needs a system that allows employers to communicate the talents they need and then prioritizes those needs using an orderly system permitting people to immigrate. Immigration is, as Reagan so eloquently stated, a fundamental base of American power and a true advantage in a brain-based world economy. Moreover, at America's stage of economic development, the birth rate is lower than replacement, and with improved healthcare, the mix of our population is trending older. Without immigration, we could well end up like Japan, with fewer and fewer young people being relied on to support their elders. An orderly system of legal immigration can keep our population younger. It turns out that economic development is the best form of birth control ever invented. In rural and agrarian societies, children are an economic asset in the form of farm labor and elder care. In a modern urban economy, children are an economic liability. Their care and education are costly, and although families and children bring wonderful and life-changing benefits, many couples are limiting the number of children they raise or avoiding it altogether. This makes immigration more attractive and, in many ways, necessary for economic well-being. This point is made in a recent study by William H. Frey of the Brookings Institution. According to Frey:

> The results of the 2020 census showed a 2010–20 decade-long decline in the nation's under-18 (youth) population, and a baby-boomer-fueled gain in its 65-and-older (senior) population, which called attention to the aging of the U.S. population. The new projections place an exclamation point on this. Each of the immigration scenarios except the "high" one shows declines in the nation's youth population during every year of the projection period. Moreover, the years in which the number of seniors supersedes the number of youths occur before 2030 in all scenarios. Because immigrants and their children are, on the whole, younger than the rest of the population, aging will occur more slowly as immigration levels rise. . . . Although the U.S. faces population growth and aging challenges in the decades ahead, we are still in a better position than many other developed countries such as Japan, Italy, Germany, and other European nations—due in large part to the healthy immigration levels we experienced over the past 30 to 40 years. While immigration remains a hot-button political issue that focuses on illegal immigrants and asylum seekers, it is crucial to move the discussion to a serious analysis of the importance of immigration for

> the nation's demographic and economic growth, and how broad policies such as comprehensive immigration reform can address our future needs. The new census projections should play a central role in those discussions.[4]

Globalization, supply chains, and immigration are connected to sustainability metrics and management because these are central to successfully navigating the complex global economy. Our view is that the ideological opposition to immigration has reached majority status due to illegal, unregulated migration. The economic need for labor and maintenance of global supply chains will very likely be an effective counter to xenophobia in the medium and long term.

THE CONNECTION BETWEEN ENVIRONMENTAL AND FINANCIAL RISK

Political acts such as war and physical manifestations of national conflict impact global trade and supply chains. Global warming has begun to have a similar impact due to extreme weather events and the impact of climate change on agriculture. As we note in earlier chapters, it is not always possible to connect environmental risk and financial risk. Environmental risk is not limited to climate risk. An organization that manufactures, ships, or utilizes toxic substances incurs risks from accidental or even deliberate release of these substances. Individuals, organizations, and jurisdictions that are harmed by toxic releases can sue polluters for the cost of damage, lost income, and cleanup. There are thousands of examples of these damages, as mentioned earlier in this work, with the largest and most prominent being General Electric's billion-dollar-plus expense due to polychlorinated biphenyl (PCB) pollution in the Hudson River, BP's $54 billion expense following its oil rig explosion in the Gulf of Mexico, and Norfolk Southern's toxic derailment in East Palestine, Ohio, already exceeding a billion dollars in cost. Hazardous material releases are relatively rare from American freight trains. According to the Federal Railroad Commission, in

2023, 6,686 freight cars carried hazardous materials, 691 were damaged or derailed, and 35 released materials. This is similar to the safety rate in 2015 when 7,903 freight cars carried hazardous materials, 650 were damaged or derailed, and 60 released materials.[5] The data over these years is consistent, but as East Palestine demonstrated, the potential for a major environmental risk is always present. Like a nuclear accident, the probability of an accident may be low, but the impact can be massive.

Investors do not yet know how to factor these risks into their investment decisions, but they are searching for data that will enable them to do this. That is the primary motor driving the development of sustainability metrics. Emulating financial accounting with mandatory reporting of sustainability metrics for publicly traded companies would lead to the development of generally accepted sustainability metrics. This would simplify and professionalize both measurement and reporting. The objective for investors is to understand how serious and competent management is at understanding and mitigating these risks. It is impossible to eliminate sustainability risks, but if management is ignoring this source of risk, investors have every right to be nervous.

It is unfortunate that the measurement and reporting of environmental risk have become politicized and considered by some to be outside the purview of the US Securities and Exchange Commission. Although this will set back the development of uniform reporting requirements in the United States, it will not dampen the demand by investors for this information. As noted earlier, states like California and the European Union will move ahead and implement their own reporting requirements, beginning with greenhouse gas emission disclosure. Companies doing business in California and Europe will still need to comply with these rules. Moreover, although environmental risk does not always correlate with financial risk, as environmental risks grow, their financial impact will grow as well.

The profile of environmental risk is growing because the probability of being in the pathway of destruction has grown. America's pattern of development is characterized by a large number of single-family homes, and as the population has grown and spread out to cover the landscape, extreme weather events and toxic releases that might have missed population centers years ago now hit them. Homes and businesses are damaged and human health is impacted, which then results in increased financial risk. The massive wildfires in Los Angeles in early 2025 were an example of an extreme weather event that, half a century ago, would have caused little damage to human settlements. The huge financial impact of that disaster should not be seen as a one-off exception but a harbinger of our future on a warmer and more crowded planet.

MEASUREMENT, MANAGEMENT, AND RISK

As indicated throughout this work, we are advocating for more thoughtful, mindful management. This requires data and the production of measures. Our view is that data-driven management enables decision-making that more fully projects risk. Modern management uses focus groups and public opinion data to understand consumers and, in some cases, is able to refine projections so precisely that they can determine the optimal size of production runs. What is key is building the organizational capacity to develop and conduct measurement, report measures, and analyze the impact of these data on organizational operations.

Data and measurement are necessary, but without management that knows how to utilize it, data is far from sufficient. The use of data in decision-making requires that information is shared throughout the organization and that potential problems and risks are exposed to the largest number of people feasible. Managers often try to hide data and potential problems. They do this out of a misguided sense of "need to know" and also in the equally misguided hope that the problem will evaporate on its own. Key performance indicators often provide senior management with information from middle managers and staff on the causes and effects of the data that these less-senior folks get to see but that may be less visible to senior management.

Discussion and brainstorming are critical, but so too is data-driven strategic thinking and action-oriented decision-making based on that data-driven strategy. We have often seen paralysis through analysis. This is when management refuses to stimulate action based on performance data and instead asks for more data or an even more refined analysis. Action-oriented performance data can tend toward quick and dirty analysis, leading to pilot efforts to change approach. Measurement and analysis are vital, but only if they are used to influence decisions in real time.

We believe that sustainability metrics are a new and vital element of every organization's key performance indicators. They should be integrated into that larger system and not separated from it. Sustainability metrics should also be integrated into management decision-making and not segregated into a separate basket for sustainability decision-making. That said, we recognize that sustainability indicators and management are an organizational innovation that, over the next decade or so, requires distinct reporting requirements, annual reports, and likely organizational capacity for sustainability. Investors and regulators are expecting distinct measures and reports, and it makes sense for organizations to respond to these stakeholders.

Sustainability management is the next stage in the evolution of effective organizational management, and it is unstoppable. The political world in Washington may dismantle policies that protect the natural environment, but the real world of corporations, local governments, and institutions must deal with a more complex, interconnected economic environment and must be mindful of their organizations' impact on the world and the world's impact on their organizations. Declaring that climate change is a hoax does not change the fact of a warming planet or its impact on us.

As we have noted throughout this work, a steady improvement in the field of organizational management has occurred over the last century and a half. In the twentieth century, we saw the development of mass production, just-in-time inventory control, global supply chains, sophisticated human resource and team management, accounting and financial management, information and performance management, total quality management, and now sustainability management. Before the Securities and Exchange Commission was begun by Franklin D. Roosevelt in 1933, there were no rules for corporate financial reporting, and accounting was mainly focused on personal income tax compliance. Most organizations lacked chief financial officers, and organizational financial control systems were a mid-twentieth-century management innovation. Before low-cost computing, low-cost internet, and cell communication, it was difficult to track organizational performance—other than monitoring revenues and expenditures. Today, every well-managed organization tracks key performance indicators and adjusts management decisions in response to data. Technology has increased the productive capacity of organizations and the demands made on senior management to understand, improve, and guide performance. Sustainability management is the latest set of practices designed to help management cope with a more crowded and resource-strained planet.

The world and the global economy are increasingly complex and interdependent. Navigating that complexity requires creative and innovative strategic thinking and care in understanding the causes and effects of organizational behavior. Organizations that have incorporated sustainability into their management routines tend to be careful and conscious of their actions. Sustainability is a means toward the goals of organizations, not a self-justifying principle of an ideology of "correct behavior." Environmental sustainability should now be seen as a subfield of sustainability management, which today includes issues such as management and staff diversity, transparent organizational governance, and the organization's impact on its surrounding community or communities. This is not "woke management" but *mindful* management. It should not be undertaken for symbolic purposes but to improve an organization's performance.

The notion of diversity and inclusion as an ideology rather than as a management principle relates to how diversity is defined and conceptualized. As a management principle, diversity is a *means* and not an *end*. Similarly, a concern for environmental impact is also utilized as a cost-cutting measure to save the costs of energy, waste management, and water and to reduce the *financial* risks of environmental liability. Environmental awareness also drives organizations to plan for the impact of extreme weather events, which can disrupt facilities, supply chains, and customers.

The reason that the profession of sustainability management will continue to progress is because it transcends politics and is deeply related to organizational effectiveness. Politicians may deny climate science and other facts, but people managing organizations do not have the luxury of ignoring reality. If your business site is flooded by an extreme weather event or is at risk of damage from such an event, you'd better have a plan B to continue operations in another location. If your competitor has invested in solar energy and generates revenues from recycling organic waste but you keep paying higher fuel bills and waste disposal fees, then your cost structure will suffer, and your competitive position will as well. If your competitor recruits immigrants to its workforce and you don't, your organization will confront costly labor shortages that could have been avoided.

Sustainability management is simply an effort to develop analytic methods and organizational practices designed to succeed in a more technologically complex, crowded world of finite resources. In some cases, the environmental, social, and governance (ESG) issues being addressed are not central to organizational success but, like many best management principles, are used by investors to judge the quality of management. In a world of limitless information, people and institutions investing capital look for a wide variety of indicators of success. Yes, EBITA (earnings before interest, taxes, and amortization), revenues, expenditures, and market share are key. But investors also look for information on the organization's competence, prospects, and strategy. They are trying to assess the risk to their capital. They know that environmental risk and the risk from climate-accelerated extreme weather events are real. Investors want to know if the organization's strategy accounts for these factors.

In other words, sustainability management is a response to a set of objective conditions. This includes the impact of pollution on human health and on the ability of our communities to withstand and recover from natural disasters. These conditions are real and not imagined. Ideology is irrelevant. In a more positive light, our culture is undergoing change as young people growing up in a more polluted and warming world are determined to reduce the environmental impact of the organizations they work for. One of our favorite examples of this took place in 2024 when a team at Amazon conducted an analysis and pilot project to develop an alternative to the little plastic bubbles that are used to protect products being shipped. They developed a paper alternative to plastic. They discovered a way to pack goods in paper that lowered package cost, lowered environmental impact, and did a better job of protecting products. That type of mindfulness and analysis is a wonderful example of sustainability management in action. Each day, organizational creativity is being unleashed to encourage environmental sustainability and closer relations with neighbors and to ensure that management decisions are not victims of groupthink and a lack of diverse perspectives.

This book has been an effort to connect sustainability metrics to sustainability management, which in our view deeply involves an understanding and management of the environmental risks and opportunities presented to every organization. We are encouraged by the cultural shift we are seeing in management to account for sustainability factors in routine decision-making. We look forward to the time when sustainability indicators are as fully integrated into decision-making as financial and nonfinancial performance indicators are today.

ACKNOWLEDGMENTS

Steven Cohen wishes to acknowledge his long-time colleague and friend Bill Eimicke for joining on another intellectual journey that resulted in this volume and to Professor Guo Dong for agreeing to put up with both Bill and Steve on this project. Both Bill and Steve have worked with Professor Guo Dong for over a decade, and he is a brilliant and talented scholar. Steve also thanks his many faculty colleagues at the School of International and Public Affairs and the School of Professional Studies, as well as the thousands of alums he has taught since arriving at Columbia in 1981. He is grateful for the support of his two deans, Keren Yarhi-Milo of Columbia's School of International and Public Affairs and Troy Eggers of the School of Professional Studies. He is also grateful for the brilliant staff work of Sarah Howard and Tal Henig-Hadar and their interns Radhika Ajayan, Enzo Cremers, Diamond Kifle, Heonjae Lee, and Lizet Ruiz Gonzalez. The intellectual debts go back a long way to SUNY Buffalo professors Marc Tipermas and Lester Milbrath. Les taught Steven environmental policy and political participation, and Marc taught him management. Marc brought Steve to Environmental Protection Agency, ICF, and Willdan and introduced him to Tom Brisbin and Mike Beiber, who Steve acknowledges for teaching about private management and the role played by the Securities and

Exchange Commission. Steve also acknowledges his loving family: his wife Donna Fishman, daughters Gabriella and Ariel, and their families, Eitan, Noa, Adi, Yael, Lily, Beka, Rob, and Penny. Steve also acknowledges his siblings: Judith, Robby, and Myra.

William Eimicke wishes to acknowledge his colleague and frequent coauthor Steve Cohen, who taught him more about sustainability management than he thought was possible and for really making sustainability an essential component of effective management. He is grateful to Guo Dong for his friendship and for teaching him so much about the realities of management in twenty-first-century China. He is grateful for the visionary leadership of his School of International and Public Affairs dean Keren Yarhi-Milo and for the support of his faculty colleagues and the entire Picker Center team. Nuoya Wu, his visiting scholar, provided substantial research and analysis for his contribution to the book. Steve Fulop, Steve Goldsmith, Tish James and his daughter Annemarie Eimicke, and colleagues Joe Pfeifer and Colleen Fitzpatrick shared essential lessons of learning how sustainability management works and doesn't work in city government. And he thanks his wife, Karen Murphy, who every day provides an example of how you must never lose your North Star of doing the right thing—and that if you work hard enough, long enough, the right things will happen.

Guo Dong wishes to acknowledge his long-time mentors, friends, and colleagues Steven Cohen and Bill Eimicke, who invited him to write this book together. He is indebted to Steve, who introduced him to the field of sustainability more than a decade ago and with whom he coauthored another book on sustainable cities. He is forever grateful to Bill, who brought him to Columbia and taught him everything about management over the past two decades. He would also like to thank his close colleagues Satyajit Bose, Anyi Wang, Christoph Meinrenken, Tal Henig-Hadar, and Sarah Howard at the Research Program on Sustainability Policy and Management of the Columbia Climate School, as well as Radhika Ajayan for providing research assistance. He is also grateful for the support of Troy Eggers, the dean of the School of Professional Studies, and our senior associate dean Erik Nelson. He has to acknowledge Professor Zhu Dajian of Tongji University in Shanghai, a preeminent scholar in sustainability in China, with whom he had passionate discussions about topics explored in this book. Last but certainly not least, he wishes to acknowledge the support of mom and dad for their endless encouragement throughout all his endeavors.

NOTES

PREFACE

1. Peter F. Drucker, *Managing in a Time of Great Change* (Routledge, 2016).

2. Max Zahn, "Corporations Struggle on Climate Goals amid Backlash Over 'Woke Capitalism,' Experts Say," *ABC News*, April 21, 2024, https://abcnews.go.com/US/corporations-struggle-climate-goals-amid-backlash-woke-capitalism/story?id=109261960.

3. Eva Moskowitz, "America's Business Community Is AWOL in Local Politics," *Wall Street Journal*, October 27, 2023, https://www.wsj.com/articles/americas-business-community-is-awol-in-local-politics-unions-labor-workers-a6c4d0ce.

4. Sasmoko Sasmoko et al., "How Do Industrial Ecology, Energy Efficiency, and Waste Recycling Technology (Circular Economy) Fit Into China's Plan to Protect the Environment? Up to Speed," *Recycling* 7, no. 6 (2022): 83, https://doi.org/10.3390/recycling7060083.

5. US Securities and Exchange Commission, "SEC Adopts Rules to Enhance and Standardize Climate-Related Disclosures for Investors," press release, March 6, 2024, https://www.sec.gov/newsroom/press-releases/2024-31.

6. Alex Tabibi, "Solar Energy and the Circular Economy: A Perfect Match," Green.org, January 30, 2024, https://green.org/2024/01/30/solar-energy-and-the-circular-economy-a-perfect-match/.

7. Bill Myers, "The Battle Against ESG Moves to US Courts," Private Funds CFO, April 29, 2024, https://www.privatefundscfo.com/the-battle-against-esg-moves-to-us-courts/.

8. Stefan Holzheuser, Jordan Hairabedian, and Juliette De Valence, "New Developments to the CSRD: What Are the Implications for Non-financial Disclosures?," Ecoact, October 13, 2023, https://eco-act.com/blog/csrd-non-financial-disclosure-in-eu/.

9. Dieter Holger, "At Least 10,000 Foreign Companies to Be Hit by EU Sustainability Rules," *Wall Street Journal*, April 5, 2023, https://www.wsj.com/articles/at-least-10-000-foreign-companies-to-be-hit-by-eu-sustainability-rules-307a1406.

10. Zeke Hausfather, Henri F. Drake, Tristan Abbott, and Gavin A. Schmidt, "Evaluating the Performance of Past Climate Model Projections," *Geophysical Research Letters* 47, no. 1 (2019), https://doi.org/10.1029/2019gl085378.

11. UN Environment Programme (UNEP), "Five Drivers of the Nature Crisis," UNEP, December 8, 2022, https://www.unep.org/news-and-stories/story/five-drivers-nature-crisis.

12. Martha Cristina Linares-Rodríguez, Nicolás Gambetta, and María Antonia García-Benau, "Carbon Management Strategy Effects on the Disclosure and Efficiency of Carbon Emissions: A Study of Colombian Companies' Context and Inherent Characteristics," *Journal of Cleaner Production* 365 (September, 2022): 132850, https://doi.org/10.1016/j.jclepro.2022.132850.

13. Bruce Hamilton, "Florida Is One of States Most At-Risk as Financial Costs of Climate Change Climb," WJXT, November 15, 2023, https://www.news4jax.com/news/local/2023/11/15/florida-is-one-of-states-most-at-risk-as-financial-costs-of-climate-change-climb/.

14. "12 US States Are Planning to Ban the Sale of Gas-Powered Cars," CNET, https://www.cnet.com/home/electric-vehicles/states-banning-new-gas-powered-cars/.

15. Neal E. Boudette and Coral Davenport, "G.M. Will Sell Only Zero-Emission Vehicles by 2035," *New York Times*, January 28, 2021, https://www.nytimes.com/2021/01/28/business/gm-zero-emission-vehicles.html.

16. "EPA Says More Data Needed to Assess Impact of $1.7B Hudson River Cleanup," *AP News*, July 10, 2024, https://apnews.com/article/hudson-river-cleanup-pcbs-epa-3b65a9b5ecf6e546deb4a384f3699969.

17. National Oceanic and Atmospheric Administration, "Deepwater Horizon Oil Spill Settlements: Where the Money Went," NOAA, 2010, https://www.noaa.gov/explainers/deepwater-horizon-oil-spill-settlements-where-money-went.

18. Russell Hotten, "Volkswagen: The Scandal Explained," *BBC News*, 2015, https://www.bbc.com/news/business-34324772.

19. Dieter Holger and Fabiana Negrin Ochoa, "Companies Grapple with Sustainability Data," *Wall Street Journal*, October 13, 2020, https://www.wsj.com/articles/companies-grapple-with-sustainability-data-11602621618.

20. General Motors, "2023 Sustainability Report: Journey to Zero," 2023, https://www.gm.com/commitments/sustainability.

1. PERFORMANCE MEASUREMENT AND PERFORMANCE MANAGEMENT

1. Steven Cohen and William B. Eimicke, *Management Fundamentals* (Columbia University Press, 2019).

2. Cohen and Eimicke, *Management Fundamentals.*

3. Mohamed Zairi and Paul Leonard, *Practical Benchmarking: The Complete Guide* (Springer Science, 1996).

4. Cohen and Eimicke, *Management Fundamentals.*

5. Cohen and Eimicke, *Management Fundamentals.*

6. Cohen and Eimicke, *Management Fundamentals.*

7. Peter Drucker, *The Daily Drucker* (Routledge, 2004).

8. Drucker, *The Daily Drucker.*

9. Erik Brynjolfsson and Kristina McElheran, "The Rapid Adoption of Data-Driven Decision-Making," *American Economic Review* 106, no. 5 (May 1, 2016): 133–39.

10. Peter Drucker, *The Practice of Management* (William Heinemann, 1955).

11. Drucker, *The Practice of Management*; George S. Odiorne, *MBO ii: A System of Managerial Leadership for the 80s* (Fearon Pitman, 1979); William J. Reddin, *Effective MBO for Irish Managers* (Mount Salus, 1974).

12. Barbara Dewey, "Aligning Work and Rewards," *Management Review* 84, no. 2 (1995), https://www.proquest.com/docview/206682899/abstract/8AB021F3575E41A4PQ/1.

13. David Parmenter, *Key Performance Indicators: Developing, Implementing, and using Winning KPIs* (Wiley, 2015).

14. Cohen and Eimicke, *Management Fundamentals.*

15. Herman Aguinis, Performance Management (Pearson Education, 2009); Steven L. Thomas and Robert D. Bretz, "Research and Practice in Performance Appraisal: Evaluating Employee Performance in America's Largest Companies," *S.A.M. Advanced Management Journal* 59, no. 2 (March 22, 1994): 28–35, https://www.questia.com/library/journal/1G1-15703609/research-and-practice-in-performance-appraisal-evaluating.

16. Drucker, *The Daily Drucker.*

17. Peter Ferdinand Drucker and Joseph A. Maciariello, *Management* (Collins, 2008).

18. Drucker, *The Daily Drucker.*

19. Hans-Gerd Ridder, Erk P. Piening, and Alina McCandless Baluch, "The Third Way Reconfigured: How and Why Nonprofit Organizations Are Shifting Their Human Resource Management," VOLUNTAS International Journal of Voluntary and Nonprofit Organizations 23, no. 3 (September 28, 2011): 605–35, https://doi.org/10.1007/s11266-011-9219-z; Marlene Walk, Heike Schinnenburg, and Femida Handy, "Missing in Action: Strategic Human Resource

Management in German Nonprofits," *VOLUNTAS International Journal of Voluntary and Nonprofit Organizations* 25, no. 4 (June 13, 2013): 991–1021, https://doi.org/10.1007/s11266-013-9380-7.

20. Avraham N. Kluger and Angelo DeNisi, "The Effects of Feedback Interventions on Performance: A Historical Review, a Meta-analysis, and a Preliminary Feedback Intervention Theory," *Psychological Bulletin* 119, no. 2 (March 1, 1996): 254–84, https://doi.org/10.1037/0033-2909.119.2.254.

21. Sally Selden and Jessica E. Sowa, "Performance Management and Appraisal in Human Service Organizations: Management and Staff Perspectives," *Public Personnel Management* 40, no. 3 (September 1, 2011): 251–64, https://doi.org/10.1177/009102601104000305.

22. Selden and Sowa, "Performance Management and Appraisal in Human Service Organizations."

23. John R. Deckop and Carol C. Cirka, "The Risk and Reward of a Double-Edged Sword: Effects of a Merit Payprogram on Intrinsic Motivation," *Nonprofit and Voluntary Sector Quarterly* 29, no. 3 (September 1, 2000): 400–418, https://doi.org/10.1177/0899764000293003.

24. Alice Robineau, Marc Ohana, and Sophie Swaton, "The Challenges of Implementing High Performance Work Practices in the Nonprofit Sector," *Journal of Applied Business Research* 31, no. 1 (December 15, 2014): 103, https://doi.org/10.19030/jabr.v31i1.8994.

25. Thomas W. Scott and P. Tiessen, "Performance Measurement and Managerial Teams," *Accounting Organizations and Society* 24, no. 3 (April 1, 1999): 263–85, https://doi.org/10.1016/s0361-3682(98)00060-9.

26. Charles J. Fombrun, Noel M. Tichy, and Mary Anne Devanna, *Strategic Human Resource Management* (Wiley, 1984).

27. Deanne N. Den Hartog, Paul Boselie, and Jaap Paauwe, "Performance Management: A Model and Research Agenda," *Applied Psychology* 53, no. 4 (September 3, 2004): 556–69, https://doi.org/10.1111/j.1464-0597.2004.00188.x.

28. Troy Kennedy and Marlene Walk, "Making Nonprofits More Effective: Performance Management and Performance Appraisals," in *The Nonprofit Human Resource Management Handbook*, ed. Jessica Word and Jessica Sowa (Routledge, 2017).

29. Gerhard Speckbacher, "The Use of Incentives in Nonprofit Organizations," *Nonprofit and Voluntary Sector Quarterly* 42, no. 5 (July 25, 2012): 1006–25, https://doi.org/10.1177/0899764012447896.

30. Ruth Rohan-Jones, "360-Degree Feedback in the Context of Leadership Development in the ADO" (CDCLMS leadership paper, Centre for Leadership Studies, Australian Defense College, Canberra, Australia, January 2004).

31. Peter Ward, *360 Degree Feedback: A Management Tool* (Jaico, 2004).

32. Monalisa Mohapatra, "360 Degree Feedback: A Review of Literature," *Research Scholar of Management KIIT University Bhubaneswar Orissa* 2, no. 1 (2015): 112–16.

33. Jyoti Kandpal, Satyawan Baroda, and Chhavi Sharma, "360 Degree Feedback Appraisals—An Innovative Approach of Performance Management System," *International Journal of Management and Information Technology* 1, no. 2 (December 19, 2018): 53–66, https://doi.org/10.24297/ijmit.v1i2.1447.

34. Fred Nickols, "Performance Appraisal: Weighed and Found Wanting in the Balance," *Journal for Quality and Participation* 30, no. 1 (2007): 13–16, 47, http://ezproxy.cul.columbia.edu/login?url=https://www.proquest.com/scholarly-journals/performance-appraisal-weighed-found-wanting/docview/219109060/se-2.

35. Ward, *360 Degree Feedback.*

36. John C. Flanagan, "The Critical Incident Technique," *Psychological Bulletin* 51, no. 4 (1954): 327–58, https://doi.org/10.1037/h0061470.

37. Roderik F. Viergever, "The Critical Incident Technique: Method or Methodology?," *Qualitative Health Research* 29, no. 7 (January 2, 2019): 1065–79, https://doi.org/10.1177/1049732318813112.

38. Charles O'Reilly, "Corporations, Culture, and Commitment: Motivation and Social Control in Organizations," *California Management Review* 31, no. 4 (July 1, 1989): 9–25, https://doi.org/10.2307/41166580.

39. Rob Goffee and Gareth Jones, "What Holds the Modern Company Together?," *Harvard Business Review*, August 1, 2014, https://hbr.org/1996/11/what-holds-the-modern-company-together.

40. Katarzyna Szczepańska-Woszczyna, "The Importance of Organizational Culture for Innovation in the Company," *Forum Scientiae Oeconomia* 2, no. 3 (2014), https://ojs.wsb.edu.pl/index.php/fso/article/view/121.

41. Constantine Kontoghiorghes, "Linking High Performance Organizational Culture and Talent Management: Satisfaction/Motivation and Organizational Commitment as Mediators," *International Journal of Human Resource Management* 27, no. 16 (October 7, 2015): 1833–53, https://doi.org/10.1080/09585192.2015.1075572.

42. Dorota Grego-Planer, "The Relationship Between Organizational Commitment and Organizational Citizenship Behaviors in the Public and Private Sectors," *Sustainability* 11, no. 22 (November 14, 2019): 6395, https://doi.org/10.3390/su11226395.

43. John R. Graham et al., "Corporate Culture: Evidence from the Field," Journal of Financial Economics 146, no. 2 (September 7, 2022): 552–93, https://doi.org/10.1016/j.jfineco.2022.07.008; Bro Uttal, "The Corporate Culture Vultures," *Fortune*, November 8, 2024, https://fortune.com/article/the-corporate-culture-vultures/.

44. Robert S. Kaplan and David P. Norton, *The Balanced Scorecard: Translating Strategy into Action* (Harvard Business School Press, 1996).

2. SUSTAINABILITY METRICS AND THE TRANSITION TO SUSTAINABILITY MANAGEMENT

1. Dieter Holger and Fabiana Negrin Ochoa, "Companies Grapple with Sustainability Data," *Wall Street Journal*, October 13, 2020, https://www.wsj.com/articles/companies-grapple-with-sustainability-data-11602621618.

2. Amir Hossein Rahdari and Ali Asghar Anvary Rostamy, "Designing a General Set of Sustainability Indicators at the Corporate Level," *Journal of Cleaner Production* 108 (December 2015): 757–71, https://doi.org/10.1016/j.jclepro.2015.05.108

3. Massimiliano Cerciello, Francesco Busato, and Simone Taddeo, "The Effect of Sustainable Business Practices on Profitability. Accounting for Strategic Disclosure," *Corporate Social Responsibility and Environmental Management* 30, no. 2 (2022), https://doi.org/10.1002/csr.2389.

4. Daniel Arenas, Josep M. Lozano, and Laura Albareda, "The Role of NGOs in CSR: Mutual Perceptions among Stakeholders," *Journal of Business Ethics* 88, no. 1 (2009): 175–97, https://doi.org/10.1007/s10551-009-0109-x.

5. J. David Goodman, "Amazon Pulls Out of Planned New York City Headquarters," *New York Times*, February 14, 2019, https://www.nytimes.com/2019/02/14/nyregion/amazon-hq2-queens.html.

6. Gary Richardson, Alejandro Komai, Michael Gou, and Daniel Park, "Stock Market Crash of 1929 | Federal Reserve History," *Federal Reserve History*, November 22, 2013, https://www.federalreservehistory.org/essays/stock-market-crash-of-1929.

7. Ellen Terrell, "Research Guides: National Recovery Administration (NRA) and the New Deal: A Resource Guide: The New Deal," *Library of Congress*, https://guides.loc.gov/national-recovery-administration/new-deal.

8. NASA and UNEP Global Environmental Alert Service (GEAS), "One Planet, How Many People? A Review of Earth's Carrying Capacity," June 2012, https://na.unep.net/geas/archive/pdfs/GEAS_Jun_12_Carrying_Capacity.pdf.

9. Raya Muttarak and Joshua Wilde, eds. *The World at 8 Billion* (Population Council, 2022).

10. Hazel Ilango, *An Unregulated ESG Rating System Reveals Its Flaws* (Institute for Energy Economics and Financial Analysis, May 2, 2023), https://ieefa.org/resources/unregulated-esg-rating-system-reveals-its-flaws.

11. Steven A. Cohen, *Sustainability Management: Lessons from and for New York City, America, and the Planet* (Columbia University Press, 2014).

12. Lydia Saad, "ESG Not Making Waves with American Public," Gallup, May 22, 2023, https://news.gallup.com/poll/506171/esg-not-making-waves-american-public.aspx.

13. Todd Rokita, "'ESG Investing' Is a Leftist Power Grab by Another Name," *Washington Examiner*, July 11, 2022, https://www.washingtonexaminer.com/opinion/380184/esg-investing-is-a-leftist-power-grab-by-another-name/.

14. Mario J. Donate, Emilio Ruiz-Monterrubio, Jesús D. Sánchez de Pablo, and Isidro Peña, "Total Quality Management and High-Performance Work Systems for Social Capital Development," *Journal of Intellectual Capital* 21, no. 1 (2019): 87–114, https://doi.org/10.1108/jic-07-2018-0116.

15. Francis Menton, "The Devastation of New York City's Economy," *Manhattan Contrarian*, https://www.manhattancontrarian.com/blog/2016/5/18/the-devastation-of-new-york-citys-economy.

16. JENKS2026, "Nanotechnology in Solar Cells: The Future of Solar Energy," Green.org, 2024, https://green.org/2024/01/30/nanotechnology-in-solar-cells-the-future-of-solar-energy/.

17. Dhananjay K. Pandey and Richa Mishra, "Towards Sustainable Agriculture: Harnessing AI for Global Food Security," *Artificial Intelligence in Agriculture* 12 (April 2024), https://doi.org/10.1016/j.aiia.2024.04.003.

18. Joseph M. Juran, "What Japan Taught Us About Quality," *Washington Post*, August 15, 1993, https://www.washingtonpost.com/archive/business/1993/08/15/what-japan-taught-us-about-quality/271f2822-b70d-4491-b942-4954caa710f8/.

19. Phyllis A. Genther, "Consolidation and Expansion," in *A History of Japan's Government-Business Relationship: The Passenger Car Industry* (University of Michigan Press, 1990), http://www.jstor.org/stable/10.3998/mpub.18703.8.

20. American Society for Quality, "Deming's 14 Points: Total Quality Management Principles," American Society for Quality, 2019, https://asq.org/quality-resources/total-quality-management/deming-points.

21. Rick LeBlanc, "Save Money with Solar Energy for Your Business," LiveAbout, June 25, 2019, https://www.liveabout.com/save-money-with-solar-energy-for-your-business-4108504.

22. Murillo Vetroni Barros et al., "Circular Economy as a Driver to Sustainable Businesses," *Cleaner Environmental Systems* 2, no. 2(2020): 100006, https://doi.org/10.1016/j.cesys.2020.100006.

23. "SEC Adopts Climate Change Disclosure Rules; Court Imposes Temporary Stay," White & Case, March 21, 2024, https://www.whitecase.com/insight-alert/sec-adopts-climate-change-disclosure-rules-court-imposes-temporary-stay.

24. Governance and Accountability Institute, "92 Percent of S&P 500® Companies and 70 Percent of Russell 1000® Companies Published Sustainability Reports in 2020, G&A Institute Research Shows," *GlobeNewswire*, November 16, 2021, https://www.globenewswire.com/news-release/2021/11/16/2335435/0/en/92-of-S-P-500-Companies-and-70-of-Russell-1000-Companies-Published-Sustainability-Reports-in-2020-G-A-Institute-Research-Shows.html.

25. "Infrastructure Investment and Jobs Act: Implementation and Key Resources," National Conference of State Legislatures, 2022, https://www.ncsl.org/state-federal/infrastructure-investment-and-jobs-act-implementation-and-key-resources.

26. "California Municipal Green Bond Issuance Passes $5 Billion: New US Green Finance Record," *Climate Bonds Initiative*, November 30, 2017, https://

www.climatebonds.net/2017/11/california-municipal-green-bond-issuance-passes-5-billion-new-us-green-finance-record.

27. "Solar Energy vs. Fossil Fuels: Comparing the Costs and Benefits," Solar Technologies, July 17, 2023, https://solartechnologies.com/solar-energy-vs-fossil-fuels-comparing-the-costs-and-benefits/.

28. Alicia Wallace, "As the CEO of Land O'Lakes, She's Changing the Rules of American Farming," *WSIL-TV*, June 25, 2024, https://www.wsiltv.com/news/consumer/as-the-ceo-of-land-o-lakes-she-s-changing-the-rules-of-american-farming/article_7abc44fb-9418-5c77-bcb6-8a352e8d2566.

3. INTEGRATING SUSTAINABILITY METRICS INTO PERFORMANCE MEASUREMENT AND FINANCIAL PERFORMANCE

1. Satyajit Bose, Guo Dong, and Anna Simpson, *The Financial Ecosystem: The Role of Finance in Achieving Sustainability* (Springer Nature, 2019).

2. Bose et al., *The Financial Ecosystem.*

3. Louis Dembitz Brandeis, *Other People's Money and How the Bankers Use It* (F.A. Stokes, 1914).

4. Bose et al., *The Financial Ecosystem.*

5. John Elkington, "Towards the Sustainable Corporation: Win-Win-Win Business Strategies for Sustainable Development," *California Management Review* 36, no. 2 (January 1, 1994): 90–100, https://doi.org/10.2307/41165746.

6. Guo Dong and Kelsie DeFrancia, "Institute for Sustainable Communities: Environment, Health and Safety Training Program Review—Research Projects—Columbia Climate School," Earth Institute, Columbia University, 2015, https://people.climate.columbia.edu/projects/view/1014.

7. United Nations, "Transforming Our World: The 2030 Agenda for Sustainable Development," 2015, https://sdgs.un.org/2030agenda.

8. United Nations Global Compact, Global Reporting Initiative, and World Business Council for Sustainable Development, "Reporting on the Sustainable Development Goals: A Practical Guide for Business," 2018, https://www.unglobalcompact.org/docs/publications/Reporting_on_the_SDGS.pdf.

9. Global Reporting Initiative, "Sector Program," 2025, https://www.globalreporting.org/standards/sector-program/.

10. Bose et al., *The Financial Ecosystem.*

11. "Integrated Reporting Framework," Integrated Reporting, 2013, https://integratedreporting.org/resource/international-ir-framework/.

12. Bob Herz and Jean Rogers, "Measuring What Matters: Industry Specificity Helps Companies and Investors Gain Traction on Sustainability," *Journal of Applied Corporate Finance* 28, no. 2 (2016):34–38, https://doi.org/10.1111/jacf.12172.

13. Sustainability Accounting Standards Board (SASB), "Exploring Materiality—SASB," December 18, 2024, https://materiality.sasb.org/.

14. Robert S. Kaplan and David P. Norton, *The Balanced Scorecard: Translating Strategy Into Action* (Harvard Business Press, 1996).

15. Frank Figge, Tobias Hahn, Stefan Schaltegger, and Marcus Wagner, "The Sustainability Balanced Scorecard—Linking Sustainability Management to Business Strategy," *Business Strategy and the Environment* 11, no. 5 (September 1, 2002): 269–84, https://doi.org/10.1002/bse.339.

16. Anna Eifert and Christian Julmi, "Challenges and How to Overcome Them in the Formulation and Implementation Process of a Sustainability Balanced Scorecard (SBSC)," *Sustainability* 14, no. 22 (November 10, 2022): 14816, https://doi.org/10.3390/su142214816.

17. Robert G. Eccles, Ioannis Ioannou, and George Serafeim, "The Impact of Corporate Sustainability on Organizational Processes and Performance," *Management Science* 60, no. 11 (2014): 2835–57, https://www.hbs.edu/ris/Publication%20Files/SSRN-id1964011_6791edac-7daa-4603-a220-4a0c6c7a3f7a.pdf.

18. Jeremy Nicholls, Eilis Lawlor, Eva Neitzert, and Tim Goodspeed, "A Guide to Social Return on Investment," *The SROI Network*, 2012, https://docs.adaptdev.info/lib/IB6EPT5U.

19. Nicholls et al., "A Guide to Social Return on Investment."

20. Rodrigo Pizarro, "Natural Capital Accounting for Integrated Climate Change Policies," Department of Economic and Social Affairs, United Nations, 2020, https://seea.un.org/content/natural-capital-accounting-integrated-climate-change-policies.

21. Ian J. Bateman et al., "Bringing Ecosystem Services Into Economic Decision-Making: Land Use in the United Kingdom," *Science* 341, no. 6141 (July 4, 2013): 45–50, https://doi.org/10.1126/science.1234379.

22. "Integrated Reporting Framework," Integrated Reporting, 2013, https://integratedreporting.org/resource/international-ir-framework/.

23. Hannah Dithrich, "Sizing the Impact Investing Market," Global Impact Investing Network, 2019, https://thegiin.org/publication/research/impinv-market-size/.

24. Jasmine Wang et al., "Doing Well by Doing Good: An Introduction to Impact Investing," SIPA Case Collection, 2019, https://www.sipa.columbia.edu/sites/default/files/2022-11/Doing%20Well%20by%20Doing%20Good%20-%20Columbia%20Case%20Study.pdf.

25. Wang et al., "Doing Well by Doing Good."

26. Wang et al., "Doing Well by Doing Good."

27. Robert Prescott-Allen, *Barometer of Sustainability: A Method of Assessing Progress Toward Sustainable Societies* (IUCN Publications, 1995).

28. Stephan Schmidheiny and Federico J. Zorraquín, "Financing Change: The Financial Community, Eco-efficiency, and Sustainable Development," *Choice Reviews Online* 33, no. 10 (June 1, 1996): 33–5834, https://doi.org/10.5860/choice.33-5834.

29. Wathis Wackernagel and William Rees, *Our Ecological Footprint: Reducing Human Impact on the Earth*, vol. 9 (New Society, 1998).

30. Gunnar Friede, Timo Busch, and Alexander Bassen, "ESG and Financial Performance: Aggregated Evidence from More Than 2000 Empirical Studies," *Journal of Sustainable Finance and Investment* 5, no. 4 (October 2, 2015): 210–33, https://doi.org/10.1080/20430795.2015.1118917.

31. Eccles et al., "The Impact of Corporate Sustainability on Organizational Processes and Performance."

32. Hao Liang and Luc Renneboog, "On the Foundations of Corporate Social Responsibility," *Journal of Finance* 72, no. 2 (December 6, 2016): 853–910, https://doi.org/10.1111/jofi.12487.

4. INTEGRATING SUSTAINABILITY MANAGEMENT INTO ORGANIZATIONAL MANAGEMENT

1. Anike Sult, Janice Wobst, and Rainer Lueg, "The Role of Training in Implementing Corporate Sustainability: A Systematic Literature Review," *Corporate Social Responsibility and Environmental Management* 31, no. 1 (2023), https://doi.org/10.1002/csr.2560.

2. Jib Ellison and Ram Nidumolu, "Sustainable Business Initiatives Will Fail Unless Leaders Change Their Mindset," *Harvard Business Review*, November 11, 2013, https://hbr.org/2013/11/sustainable-business-initiatives-will-fail-unless-leaders-change-their-mindset.

3. Jurgita Balaisyte, "Which Sectors Are Most Affected by Climate," MSCI, May 15, 2015, https://www.msci.com/www/quick-take/which-sectors-are-most-affected/03827173296.

4. Cain Burdeau, "BP Estimates Cost of 2010 Gulf Oil Spill at $61.6 Billion," *AP News*, July 14, 2014, https://apnews.com/national-national-general-news-15247c9394684b86bafofff7fa2489c7.

5. Jonathan Franklin, "Norfolk Southern Reaches a Multimillion-Dollar Settlement Over Ohio Train Derailment," *NPR*, May 23, 2024, https://www.npr.org/2024/05/23/nx-s1-4977598/norfolk-southern-multi-million-dollar-settlement-ohio-train-derailment.

6. Tim Bajarin, "Attack of the Clones: How IBM Lost Control of the PC Market," *Forbes*, August 25, 2021, https://www.forbes.com/sites/timbajarin/2021/08/25/attack-of-the-clones-how-ibm-lost-control-of-the-pc-market/.

7. "Services, Value Added (% of GDP)—United States," World Bank, https://data.worldbank.org/indicator/NV.SRV.TOTL.ZS?locations=US.

8. J. David Goodman, "Amazon Pulls Out of Planned New York City Headquarters," *New York Times*, February 14, 2019, https://www.nytimes.com/2019/02/14/nyregion/amazon-hq2-queens.html.

9. Alex Presha and Jeremy Edwards, "Whistleblower Claims EPA Wasted Critical Time after Devastating Ohio Train Derailment," *ABC News*, May 16, 2024, https://abcnews.go.com/US/whistleblower-claims-epa-wasted-critical-time-after-devastating/story?id=110313045.

10. "SEC Stays Its Climate Rule Pending Judicial Review," KPMG, April 2024, https://kpmg.com/us/en/frv/reference-library/2024/sec-stays-its-climate-rule-pending-judicial-review.html.

11. US Securities and Exchange Commission, "SEC Adopts Rules to Enhance and Standardize Climate-Related Disclosures for Investors," March 6, 2024, https://www.sec.gov/newsroom/press-releases/2024-31.

12. US Securities and Exchange Commission, "SEC Adopts Rules to Enhance and Standardize Climate-Related Disclosures for Investors."

13. Jon McGowan, "To Survive Legal Challenges, SEC Must Remove Scope 3 from Sustainability Reporting Rule," *Forbes*, February 28, 2024, https://www.forbes.com/sites/jonmcgowan/2024/02/23/to-survive-legal-challenges-sec-must-remove-scope-3-from-sustainability-reporting-rule/.

14. Ed Ballard, "Disclosures on Nature, Climate Go Hand in Hand, Nestlé Risk Chief Says," *Wall Street Journal*, March 24, 2022, https://www.wsj.com/articles/disclosures-on-nature-climate-go-hand-in-hand-nestle-risk-chief-says-11648116000.

15. James Acton, "The Ukraine War's Lingering Nuclear Power Danger," Carnegie Endowment for International Peace, February 21, 2023, https://carnegieendowment.org/posts/2023/02/the-ukraine-wars-lingering-nuclear-power-danger?lang=en.

16. Ballard, "Disclosures on Nature, Climate Go Hand in Hand."

17. Bernard Le Foll et al., "Tobacco and Nicotine Use," *Nature Reviews Disease Primers* 8, no. 1 (2022), https://doi.org/10.1038/s41572-022-00346-w.

18. Richard Vanderford, "SEC Climate Disclosure Proposal Looms as Litigation Risk," *Wall Street Journal*, March 26, 2022, https://www.wsj.com/articles/sec-climate-disclosure-proposal-looms-as-litigation-risk-11648299600.

19. Lindsay Beltzer, "A Brief Guide to Upskilling Your Workforce in Sustainability," The Conference Board, 2024, https://www.conferenceboard.org/pdfdownload.cfm?masterProductID=50082.

20. Rick Wartzman and Kelly Tang, "Climate-Related Jobs Are a Hallmark of Better-Managed Companies," *Wall Street Journal*. July 28, 2024, https://www.wsj.com/business/c-suite/climate-change-jobs-company-management-d2f37311?mod=Searchresults_pos1&page=1.

21. Apple, "2024 Environmental Progress Report," 2024, https://www.apple.com/environment/pdf/Apple_Environmental_Progress_Report_2024.pdf.

22. Mark Gongloff, "Apple's Climate Claims Deserve Scrutiny," *Washington Post*, September 14, 2023, https://www.washingtonpost.com/business/energy/2023/09/13/iphone-apple-s-climate-claims-shouldn-t-escape-scrutiny/2bdd0c0c-5260-11ee-accf-88c266213aac_story.html.

23. Gongloff, "Apple's Climate Claims Deserve Scrutiny."

24. Christopher Marquis, "Can High-End Fashion and Sustainability Co-Exist? Chloé Has Designs on Style with Purpose," *Forbes*, November 22, 2022, https://www.forbes.com/sites/christophermarquis/2022/11/22/can-high-end-fashion-and-sustainability-co-exist-chlo-has-designs-on-style-with-purpose/.

25. Marquis, "Can High-End Fashion and Sustainability Co-Exist?"

26. Jess Cartner-Morley, "'I Never Think About Trends': Gabriela Hearst Brings Sustainability to Chloé Show," *Guardian*, March 2, 2023, https://www.theguardian.com/fashion/2023/mar/02/i-never-think-about-trends-gabriela-hearst-brings-sustainability-to-chloe-show.

27. Larry Fink, "Larry Fink CEO Letter," BlackRock, 2021, https://www.blackrock.com/corporate/investor-relations/2021-larry-fink-ceo-letter.

28. "BlackRock Inc. Stock Price and News," *Wall Street Journal*, 2024, https://www.wsj.com/market-data/quotes/blk.

29. Dawn Lim and Julie Steinberg, "BlackRock to Hold Companies and Itself to Higher Standards on Climate Risk," *Wall Street Journal*, January 14, 2020, https://www.wsj.com/articles/blackrock-shakes-up-sustainable-investing-business-following-criticism-11579000873?mod=article_inline.

30. Dawn Lim, "Larry Fink Wants to Save the World (and Make Money Doing It)," *Wall Street Journal*, January 6, 2022, https://www.wsj.com/articles/larry-fink-wants-to-save-the-world-and-make-money-doing-it-11641484864?mod=article_inline.

31. Jack Pitcher and Amrith Ramkumar, "Step Aside, ESG. BlackRock Is Doing 'Transition Investing' Now," *Wall Street Journal*, March 3, 2024, https://www.wsj.com/finance/investing/step-aside-esg-blackrock-is-doing-transition-investing-now-59df3908.

32. Shane Shifflett, "Wall Street's ESG Craze Is Fading," *Wall Street Journal*, November 19, 2023, https://www.wsj.com/finance/investing/esg-branding-wall-street-0a487105?mod=article_inline.

33. Pitcher and Ramkumar, "Step Aside, ESG."

5. ENVIRONMENT, DEI, TRANSPARENT ORGANIZATIONAL GOVERNANCE, AND COMMUNITY IMPACT: IDEOLOGY AND MANAGEMENT COMPETENCE

1. Nuoya Wu, SIPA Visiting Scholar during 2024, contributed significantly to the research and analysis on sustainability beyond environmental issues.

2. Henry George, *Progress and Poverty: An Inquiry Into the Cause of Industrial Depressions and of Increase of Want with Increase of Wealth; The Remedy*, from Cambridge Library Collection—British and Irish History, Nineteenth Century (Cambridge University Press, 2009).

3. Gro Harlem Brundtland, *Our Common Future: The World Commission on Environment and Development* (Oxford University Press, 1987), 43.

4. John Elkington, *Cannibals with Forks: The Triple Bottom Line of Twenty-First Century Business* (New Society, 1998).

5. Puneeta Goel, "Triple Bottom Line Reporting: An Analytical Approach for Corporate Sustainability," *Journal of Finance, Accounting and Management* 1, no. 1 (July 2010): 27–42, https://search.ebscohost.com/login.aspx?direct=true&AuthType=ip&db=bth&AN=61996575&site=ehost-live&scope=site.

6. "The Ten Principles," UN Global Compact, September 27, 2024, https://unglobalcompact.org/what-is-gc/mission/principles.

7. Howard W. Buffett and William B. Eimicke, *Social Value Investing: A Management Framework for Effective Partnerships* (Columbia University Press, 2018).

8. "United Nations Millennium Development Goals," United Nations, https://www.un.org/millenniumgoals/bkgd.shtml.

9. Elvis D. Achuo, Clovis Wendji Miamo, and Tii N. Nchofoung, "Energy Consumption and Environmental Sustainability: What Lessons for Posterity?," *Energy Reports* 8 (September 30, 2022): 12491–502, https://doi.org/10.1016/j.egyr.2022.09.033; Jeffrey K. Seadon, "Sustainable Waste Management Systems," *Journal of Cleaner Production* 18, no. 16–17 (2010): 1639–51; Alexis Laurent, Stig I. Olsen, and Michael Z. Hauschild, "Limitations of Carbon Footprint as Indicator of Environmental Sustainability," *Environmental Science and Technology* 46, no. 7 (2012): 4100–108.

10. M. Mohammed et al., "A Review on Achieving Sustainable Construction Waste Management Through Application of 3R (Reduction, Reuse, Recycling): A Lifecycle Approach," *IOP Conference Series Earth and Environmental Science* 476, no. 1 (April 1, 2020): 012010, https://doi.org/10.1088/1755-1315/476/1/012010.

11. Nabila Abid, Federica Ceci, Fayyaz Ahmad, and Junaid Aftab, "Financial Development and Green Innovation, the Ultimate Solutions to an Environmentally Sustainable Society: Evidence from Leading Economies," *Journal of Cleaner Production* 369 (July 30, 2022): 133223, https://doi.org/10.1016/j.jclepro.2022.133223.

12. Nicole Darnall, G. Jason Jolley, and Robert Handfield, "Environmental Management Systems and Green Supply Chain Management: Complements for Sustainability?," *Business Strategy and the Environment* 17, no. 1 (October 25, 2006): 30–45, https://doi.org/10.1002/bse.557.

13. Mohammad Jasim Uddin, Rumana Huq Luva, and Saad Md Maroof Hossain, "Impact of Organizational Culture on Employee Performance and Productivity: A Case Study of Telecommunication Sector in Bangladesh," *International Journal of Business and Management* 8, no. 2 (December 24, 2012), https://doi.org/10.5539/ijbm.v8n2p63.

14. Kevin Stainback, Donald Tomaskovic-Devey, and Sheryl Skaggs, "Organizational Approaches to Inequality: Inertia, Relative Power, and Environments," *Annual Review of Sociology* 36, no. 1 (2010): 225–47.

15. Donald Tomaskovic-Devey and Kevin Stainback, "Discrimination and Desegregation: Equal Opportunity Progress in US Private Sector Workplaces Since the Civil Rights Act," *Annals of the American Academy of Political and Social Science* 609, no. 1 (2007): 49–84.

16. Cecilia L. Ridgeway, "Why Status Matters for Inequality," *American Sociological Review* 79, no. 1 (2014): 1–16.

17. Amy C. Wilkins and Jennifer A. Pace, "Class, Race, and Emotions," in *Handbook of the Sociology of Emotions*, vol. 2, ed. J. Stets and J. Turner (Springer, 2014).

18. David A. Cotter, Joan M. Hermsen, Seth Ovadia, and Reeve Vanneman, "The Glass Ceiling Effect," *Social Forces* 80, no. 2 (2001): 655–81.

19. Steven Vallas and Emily Cummins, "Relational Models of Organizational Inequalities: Emerging Approaches and Conceptual Dilemmas," *American Behavioral Scientist* 58, no. 2 (2014): 228–55.

20. Loïc J. D. Wacquant, "For an Analytic of Racial Domination," *Political Power and Social Theory* 2 (1997): 221–34.

21. "Supported Employment Program | Global Diversity and Inclusion," Microsoft, https://www.microsoft.com/en-us/diversity/supportedemployment.

22. "Supported Employment Program | Global Diversity and Inclusion."

23. "Supported Employment Program | Global Diversity and Inclusion."

24. Nicholas Confessore, "What to Know About the University of Michigan's D.E.I. Experiment," *New York Times*, October 16, 2024, https://www.nytimes.com/2024/10/16/magazine/university-of-michigan-dei.html?searchResultPosition=1.

25. Confessore, "What to Know About the University of Michigan's D.E.I. Experiment."

26. Paul Brest and Emily J. Levine, "Opinion | D.E.I. Is Not Working on College Campuses. We Need a New Approach," *New York Times*, August 30, 2024, https://www.nytimes.com/2024/08/30/opinion/college-dei-programs-diversity.html?searchResultPosition=3.

27. Mauricio Andres Latapi Agudelo, Lara Johannsdottir, and Brynhildur Davidsdottir, "A Literature Review of the History and Evolution of Corporate Social Responsibility," *International Journal of Corporate Social Responsibility* 4, no. 1 (2019), https://doi.org/10.1186/s40991-018-0039-y.

28. Nazamul Hoque, Mohammad Rahim Uddin, Md Ibrahim, and Abdullahil Mamun, "Corporate Social Responsibilities (CSR) as a Means of Materializing Corporate Vision: A Volvo Group Approach," *Asian Social Science* 10, no. 11 (2014): 258.

29. Hildegunn Mellesmo Aslaksen, Clare Hildebrandt, and Hans Chr Garmann Johnsen, "The Long-Term Transformation of the Concept of CSR: Towards a More Comprehensive Emphasis on Sustainability," *International Journal of Corporate Social Responsibility* 6, no. 1 (2021): 11.

30. Nadia Reckmann, "What Is Corporate Social Responsibility (CSR)?," *Business News Daily*, October 3, 2024, https://www.businessnewsdaily.com/4679-corporate-social-responsibility.html.

31. Gopal K. Kanji and Parvesh K. Chopra, "Corporate Social Responsibility in a Global Economy," *Total Quality Management* 21, no. 2 (2010): 119–43.

32. Eghe R. Osagie et al., "Individual Competencies for Corporate Social Responsibility: A Literature and Practice Perspective," *Journal of Business Ethics* 135 (2016): 233–52.

33. Maimunah Ismail, "Corporate Social Responsibility and Its Role in Community Development: An International Perspective," *Journal of International Social Research* 2, no. 9 (2009): 308–18.

34. Elisabet Garriga and Domènec Melé, "Corporate Social Responsibility Theories: Mapping the Territory," *Journal of Business Ethics* 53, no. 1 (2004): 51–71.

35. Diana-Abasi Ibanga, "Is There a Social Contract Between the Firm and Community: Revisiting the Philosophy of Corporate Social Responsibility," *International Journal of Development and Sustainability* 7, no. 1 (January 1, 2018), https://philpapers.org/archive/IBAITA.pdf.

36. Zhejiang Jasan Group Co., Ltd., 2024, https://jasangroup.com/en/.

37. Khaled Saadaoui and Teerooven Soobaroyen, "An Analysis of the Methodologies Adopted by CSR Rating Agencies," *Sustainability Accounting, Management and Policy Journal* 9, no. 1 (2018): 43–62.

38. Steven Cohen, "A Renewable Resource-Based Economy Requires Public-Private Partnership," State of the Planet, March 9, 2020, https://news.climate.columbia.edu/2020/03/09/renewable-resource-based-economy-requires-public-private/.

6. MEASUREMENT AND DISCLOSURE OF CARBON AND CLIMATE RISKS

1. "EMC: Continuous Emission Monitoring Systems," US EPA, January 2, 2025, https://www.epa.gov/emc/emc-continuous-emission-monitoring-systems.

2. Isabel Wolf, Peter K. R. Holzapfel, Henning Meschede, and Matthias Finkbeiner, "On the Potential of Temporally Resolved GHG Emission Factors for Load Shifting: A Case Study on Electrified Steam Generation," *Applied Energy* 348 (July 3, 2023): 121433, https://doi.org/10.1016/j.apenergy.2023.121433.

3. Ranjini Guruprasad, Manikandan Padmanaban, and Lloyd A. Treinish, "Increasing the Spatio-Temporal Resolution of OCO2 GHG Satellite Data," *IGARSS 2022–2022 IEEE International Geoscience and Remote Sensing Symposium* 12144 (July 17, 2022): 7701–4. https://doi.org/10.1109/igarss46834.2022.9883108.

4. Lena Klaaßen and Christian Stoll, "Harmonizing Corporate Carbon Footprints," *Nature Communications* 12, no. 1 (October 22, 2021), https://doi.org/10.1038/s41467-021-26349-x.

5. Stefan Brönnimann et al., "Historical Weather Data for Climate Risk Assessment," *Annals of the New York Academy of Sciences* 1436, no. 1 (October 5, 2018): 121–37, https://doi.org/10.1111/nyas.13966.

6. Anuj Karpatne and Stefan Liess, "A Guide to Earth Science Data: Summary and Research Challenges," *Computing in Science and Engineering* 17, no. 6 (October 28, 2015): 14–18, https://doi.org/10.1109/mcse.2015.127.

7. Raffaele Albano and Aurelia Sole, "Geospatial Methods and Tools for Natural Risk Management and Communications," *ISPRS International Journal of Geo-Information* 7, no. 12 (December 2, 2018): 470, https://doi.org/10.3390/ijgi7120470.

8. "CDP Guidance and Questionnaires," CDP, 2025, https://www.cdp.net/en/guidance.

9. Ans Kolk, David Levy, and Jonatan Pinkse, "Corporate Responses in an Emerging Climate Regime: The Institutionalization and Commensuration of Carbon Disclosure," *European Accounting Review* 17, no. 4 (November 19, 2008): 719–45, https://doi.org/10.1080/09638180802489121.

10. "CDP A List Companies 2023," CDP, https://www.cdp.net/en/companies/companies-scores.

11. Mei Li, Gregory Trencher, and Jusen Asuka, "The Clean Energy Claims of BP, Chevron, ExxonMobil and Shell: A Mismatch Between Discourse, Actions and Investments," *PLoS ONE* 17, no. 2 (February 16, 2022): e0263596, https://doi.org/10.1371/journal.pone.0263596.

12. "CDP A List Companies 2023."

13. Andrew Johnston, "Climate-Related Financial Disclosures: What Next for Environmental Sustainability?," University of Oslo Faculty of Law Research Paper no. 2018-02, 2018, https://papers.ssrn.com/sol3/papers.cfm?abstract_id=3122259.

14. Dong Ding, Bin Liu, and Millicent Chang, "Carbon Emissions and TCFD Aligned Climate-Related Information Disclosures," *Journal of Business Ethics* 182, no. 4 (December 2, 2022): 967–1001, https://doi.org/10.1007/s10551-022-05292-x.

15. Dirk Otto Beerbaum, "Green Quadriga?—EU—Taxonomy, TCFD, Non-Financial-Reporting Directive and EBA ESG Pillar III/IFRS Foundation," *SSRN Electronic Journal*, January 1, 2021, https://doi.org/10.2139/ssrn.3824397.

16. Jean-Baptiste Poulle et al., "Corporate Sustainability Reporting Directive," in *EU Banking and Financial Regulation* (Elgar Financial Law and Practice, 2024), https://www.e-elgar.com/shop/gbp/eu-banking-and-financial-regulation-9781035301942.html?srsltid=AfmBOorUkcShr2aJdUYrhiP6Si9fOPb61mPsns700gOuX1wKroeSJo9R.

17. Massimiliano Celli, Simona Arduini, and Tommaso Beck, "Corporate Sustainability Reporting Directive (CSRD) and His Future Application Scenario for Italian SMEs," *International Journal of Business and Management* 19, no. 4 (June 7, 2024): 44, https://doi.org/10.5539/ijbm.v19n4p44.

18. Richard M. Frankel, S. P. Kothari, and Aneesh Raghunandan, "The Economics of ESG Disclosure Regulation," *SSRN Electronic Journal*, January 1, 2023, https://doi.org/10.2139/ssrn.4647550.

19. Frankel et al., "The Economics of ESG Disclosure Regulation."

20. CDP, CDSB, GRI, IIRC, and SASB, "Statement of Intent to Work Together Towards Comprehensive Corporate Reporting: Summary of Alignment Discussions Among Leading Sustainability and Integrated Reporting Organisations CDP, CDSB, GRI, IIRC and SASB," September 2020, https://www.globalreporting.org/media/bixjk1ud/statement-of-intent-to-work-together-towards-comprehensive-corporate-reporting.pdf.

7. CONCLUSION: ENVIRONMENTAL RISK, FINANCIAL RISK, AND EFFECTIVE MANAGEMENT IN A COMPLEX, TECHNOLOGICAL, AND GLOBAL ECONOMY

1. "COVID-19—State of the Planet," Columbia Climate School, December 16, 2022, https://news.climate.columbia.edu/tag/covid-19/.

2. John F. Kennedy and Edward M. Kennedy, *A Nation of Immigrants* (Harper Perennial, 2008).

3. Ronald Reagan, "Ronald Reagan: Immigrants—'Most Important Sources of America's Greatness,'" Presented at the White House Ceremonies, 1989, https://www.wral.com/story/ronald-reagan-immigrants-most-important-sources-of-america-s-greatness/18512339/.

4. William Frey, "New Census Projections Show Immigration Is Essential to the Growth and Vitality of a More Diverse US Population," Brookings, November 29, 2023, https://www.brookings.edu/articles/new-census-projections-show-immigration-is-essential-to-the-growth-and-vitality-of-a-more-diverse-us-population/.

5. Office of Safety Analysis, Federal Railroad Administration, "Ten Year Accident/Incident Overview," https://safetydata.fra.dot.gov/OfficeofSafety/publicsite/Query/TenYearAccidentIncidentOverview.aspx.

INDEX

GPSR Authorized Representative: Easy Access System Europe, Mustamäe tee 50, 10621 Tallinn, Estonia, gpsr.requests@easproject.com

www.ingramcontent.com/pod-product-compliance
Lightning Source LLC
Chambersburg PA
CBHW030505210326
41597CB00013B/794

* 9 7 8 0 2 3 1 2 2 0 6 7 5 *